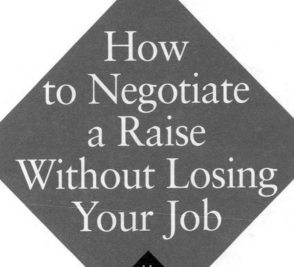

How to Negotiate a Raise Without Losing Your Job

Second Edition ◆ George M. Hartman

Former Engineering
Subcontracts Manager,
Unisys Corporation

BARRON'S

All inquiries should be addressed to:
Barron's Educational Series, Inc.
250 Wireless Boulevard
Hauppauge, New York 11788

Library of Congress Catalog Card No. 97-10311

International Standard Book No. 0-8120-9895-1

Library of Congress Cataloging-in-Publication Data
Hartman, George M.
    How to negotiate a raise without losing your job / by
George M. Hartman.
        p.   cm.
    Rev. ed. of: How to negotiate a bigger raise. ©1991.
    Includes bibliographical references and index.
    ISBN 0-8120-9895-1
    1. Executives—Salaries, etc.—United States.
2. Negotiation in business—United States.   3. Career
development—United States.   4. Success in business—United
States.   I. Hartman, George M.   How to negotiate a
bigger raise.   II. Title.
HD4965.5.U6H33   1997
650.1'2—dc21   97-10311
                                                            CIP

PRINTED IN HONG KONG
987654321

DEDICATION

This edition is dedicated to Shirley Orenstein, whose encouragement, understanding, and love helped me through some rough times.

I also dedicate this book to those managers, both new and experienced, who may need encouragement at times when dealing with their superiors or corporate officers.

I would also like to include my editor, Tracey Topper, for her avid assistance in preparation of the manuscript.

◆

"To survive and prosper in the new scary economy, you'd better understand that the rules have changed."

—Robert Reich
Former Secretary of Labor

Contents

◆

Preface

◆

The objective of this book's first edition, titled *How to Negotiate a Bigger Raise*, was to assist any middle manager in obtaining more than an average raise. Since its initial date of publication, our economy has changed. Now the word *downsizing* has become as common as the word *layoff* was in the '70s and '80s. Consequently, this second edition has been appropriately retitled: *How to Negotiate a Raise Without Losing Your Job*.

Unlike the game of golf where a golfer may take a "mulligan" to assure improving his or her drive, an employee has only one opportunity to demonstrate his or her worth. Even if you are a college-educated person, more than 25 years old, and looking forward to high earnings during your career, you will probably have butterflies in your stomach when it comes to asking for a raise.

It seems that every day we read about how giant, medium, and small-size industries are planning layoffs of a few to thousands of workers. With most of these downsizes or reorganizations, the plans, scenarios, or themes seem to be the same.

The company may still be profitable and may still dominate its industry, but its top management, in pursuing a worldwide position, believes that mergers and layoffs lead to further profitability, especially when meeting or outdistancing its competitors. Thus, the pressure is on middle managers to improve their performance. Ultimately, this improvement should aid in emphasizing their net worth and that should help not only in gaining future raises but also in retaining their positions.

In past generations, recent high school or college graduates could look forward to working for companies for security in return for loyalty. The "company person" would start at the bottom, usually in a training program, and then climb the "ladder of success." That's no longer the case. In the new world of employment we look at jobs as simply jobs. We anticipate being forced to move from job to job and learning new skills when required due to changes in the technical environment.

Because of this change in attitudes toward careers, a new chapter, You Didn't Get That Raise, Now What?, has been added to the book for considering alternate paths to take. You may contemplate changing your career, or changing your employer, or relocating—all of which may offer more opportunity for raises or promotions, or both.

All sections of the original edition of this book have been updated or amended to coincide with the theme of this revised edition. For example, Chapter 3 has been revised to include a questionnaire for assessing one's management skills and leadership qualifications. However, the primary goal of the book remains the same: to assist in getting an adequate raise.

In addition, the book has been expanded to provide more insight into developing additional assets and skills required to make you more desirable in the job market and more valuable to your company. The book also provides a new Appendix containing descriptions of computer software that is available and may be valuable for assistance to middle managers.

The key to career success today is in strengthening your qualifications so that a raise, not a layoff, is always on the horizon.

Chapter 1

Negotiate That Raise; Don't Wait for an "Automatic" Increase

"I believe that people most directly involved— whose lives and destiny are most directly affected—should always be parties to the negotiations in which their future is being decided."

—Jeane Kirkpatrick
Former U.S. Ambassador to the U.N.

So you've decided that it's time for a raise! But before taking action, you need a battle plan. Here are some things to consider:

◆ your worth, as a middle manager, to the company— specifically, why you deserve a bigger paycheck;

◆ the salary/fringe benefits limits you are willing to accept;

◆ the salary levels and policies prevailing in your company;

◆ your supervisor's probable reaction to your request;

◆ the strategies and tactics you will need to negotiate the raise you want.

Later chapters will deal with these topics in detail. The purpose of this Introduction is to encourage you to go after the raise you deserve, to introduce you to negotiation techniques, to convince you that you can learn to negotiate effectively, and to help you assess the limitations on what you can reasonably expect.

However, you must tread lightly and be extremely diplomatic, cooperative, and confident that you are a valuable asset to your company. Avoid going off half-cocked with the notion that you're a hotshot when your performance is only mediocre. Do nothing to jeopardize your job, unless you have a replacement position waiting for you.

PRINCIPLE 1

If a CEO's value is worth millions, certainly a company can well afford to reward a hard-working middle manager with an adequate raise.

1. Measuring Your Worth

A recent report by President Clinton's Council of Economic Advisors indicated that this country's economy has produced 8.5 million more nonfarm jobs than it lost since January 1993. Furthermore, roughly 60 percent of the net job growth over the past three years has been in managerial and professional positions. These additional jobs have helped neutralize somewhat the effects of corporate downsizing. Nevertheless, the report continues, those that fit in the category of higher educated middle-age managers no longer feel secure in the positions they hold.

Ask managers to describe why they feel depressed despite learning about the President's encouraging report and, without hesitation, they will usually point to the inequities of corporate salary structures—specifically, the differences between their salaries and those of their bosses. They will gripe about not getting recognition for job performance where it counts—in their wallets. In the 1980s, the CEO's average compensation increased approximately 300 percent over a ten-year period, whereas the production worker gained an average of only 50 percent.

The frustrating news these days is that managers are apt to have their salaries suppressed, whereas CEOs and top executives continue to receive enormous salaries, bonuses, and stock options. But we cannot give up the goal of earning the wages we believe we deserve. We should concentrate on getting more than adequate compensation for our performance—the more outstanding, the higher the rewards. If you fall into a certain labor category, you usually have a general idea of your salary span. However, you must do your homework to find out if there will be increases in the salary structure in the near future and also what it takes for promotional opportunity. Do not pressure your supervisor by citing executive salaries unless it's germane to your salary review.

For example, point out how more high-paying jobs are being created despite corporate downsizing, in particular in managerial and professional positions. As indicated previously, attitudes have changed; people who felt secure about their jobs, especially those who are middle-aged and well-educated, are finding themselves unemployed. Consequently, in today's environment, you have to work harder to prove yourself, demonstrating your full qualifications and worth to the company.

There are many mixed signals in industries that have downsized at the same time as they have awarded top executives—in some instances for less tangible achievements. This is quite frustrating to middle management. Downsizing may help a company improve its profits, but it may foster a "damned if you do and damned if you don't" attitude in middle managers. For example, if a middle manager does a masterful job of cost savings, he may kick himself right out of his job instead of being rewarded with more compensation, like an increase in salary or a bonus. It's possible that cost-saving techniques will result in having lower salaried personnel complete the work that needs to be done. But if this is the way a corporation rewards its skilled workers, it's time for the middle manager to find the right place for himself or herself. Fortunately, most firms recognize excellent performance as a way to measure one's worth, and, for the cited case, the manager most likely would receive a promotion or a lateral transfer to another department. Thus, we still believe that a company that is considered top-notch will award its diligent managers, especially those who prove themselves as assets to the firm. Furthermore, within limits, negotiating a decent raise is still apropos! The problem in getting this raise is that most people do not know how to do it. They are afraid of rejection and may not even try.

Generally, the smaller the firm you work for, the more flexibility you have in negotiating a raise. For example, a computer programmer employed by a small company has a better chance to negotiate a decent raise than a contract manager working for a giant organization. The smaller company can be harmed by key personnel leaving for greener pastures whereas the larger firm finds little difficulty in employing replacements. Again, the more one proves his or her net worth, the better chance of getting either a raise or promotion or both.

So where does the manager fit in? How does a company determine what a manager is worth? Who establishes what is the right salary for a particular quality of service? The subject of worth is covered in more detail in Chapter 3. Chapter 4 discusses the salary administration techniques used by the human resource departments of many companies. These techniques help in grading jobs and in evaluating performance and other relevant factors to establish salaries and salary-level ranges.

Unlike managers, CEOs and production workers can at least cope with inflation; their salaries and wages tend to keep pace with cost-of-living increases. However, when it's their turn for raises, many managers find themselves at the mercy of their bosses. When a company is doing well, its managers may receive salary increases that are reasonably comparable, in terms of percentages, to those of production workers. But when times are bad, many companies limit raises, and the managers are frequently the last to be considered. CEOs will still get their base salaries; or, if asked to resign, they may float away beneath "golden parachutes." And production workers will probably get their raises right on schedule, especially if they are unionized.

So sharpen your wits—and, of course, your negotiating skills—and get ready to do battle by showing not only what you are worth today but also what a valuable asset you have been and will be to your company and, especially, to your supervisor.

2. An Overview of Negotiation Techniques

In Jack Chapman's book, *How to Make $1,000 a Minute: Negotiating Salaries and Raises,* Richard Germann asks, "Is it true that you can negotiate anything? The answer is, 'Of course you can!' But will it do you any good? This requires a longer answer." People who are facing negotiations can be divided into three categories: those who don't try negotiating because they feel uncomfortable, don't know how, or have made up their minds it won't work; those who negotiate without plan or purpose and therefore to no effect; and those who see negotiating as a valuable skill to develop and practice conscientiously.

The art of negotiation requires skills and knowledge that come from experience, not from formal education.

Preparation for negotiation is necessary to reach a successful conclusion. Invest in your own time, away from the office, to establish what you expect to accomplish in a salary review session. Consider what you expect to achieve, while recognizing your minimum requirements. With adequate preparation, you should be able to evaluate whether a good deal was struck.

Regardless of your experience or lack of it, when applying negotiation techniques you should know when to use strategies and tactics—and how to tell them apart:

◆ *strategy* consists of the plans developed in preparation for a negotiation session;

◆ *tactics* are extemporaneous methods of reaching agreements.

Negotiation is successful when both parties profit from it. This mutual benefit should be your goal when you begin to negotiate for a pay increase. After all, you will probably be dealing with your supervisor on many other occasions if you both remain with the company.

The goal of the negotiation process is winning. Therefore, your strategy must include gaining insight into these factors: your performance and profit motivation, company needs, salary versus position, available options, and the company's financial condition. You should also consider ways to control the tempo of the negotiation without appearing to be in command.

Your negotiation skills should include the ability to communicate effectively, to observe and read people, and most important, to think on your feet. The quality of your communication is demonstrated by how well you present your case and how readily it is comprehended and accepted. You must also listen carefully to what is being said. Prior knowledge of your supervisor's personality, needs, and goals can help you to negotiate more effectively.

3. Yes, You Can Be an Effective Negotiator

What makes a negotiator effective? Whether you are negotiating for a salary increase or a contract, you should consider this question carefully. For a negotiator, the three most desirable qualities are aspiration, skill, and self-confidence. With these three (plus a dash of power, which will be discussed last), a negotiator should get the desired results.

Let's consider each of the three qualities separately.

Aspiration has a big influence on the outcome of a negotiation. The negotiator with a high level of aspiration has a strong desire to win. Conversely, fear of failure is characteristic of a low aspiration level.

Skill includes knowledge of negotiation techniques— strategies and tactics—and good communication. (Skill techniques necessary to negotiate are described in Chapter 7.)

Self-confidence is usually acquired through maturation and experience. A negotiator must think well of him- or herself in order to project a favorable impression.

A moment's reflection reveals that these three important qualities are closely interrelated. If you have high *aspiration* to succeed, you will recognize the need for the negotiating *skills* that will enable you to prevail. In turn, by acquiring these techniques, you will greatly increase your level of *self-confidence.* And from all three will come a heady sense of *power*—a conviction that you can control events and people to achieve your purpose.

As an effective negotiator, you will also need other skills and qualities:

◆ *Ability to plan:* Perhaps the most productive time in the negotiation process is spent in planning, including the capability of showing your worth and being prepared with an activity log. (Worth and the activity log are covered in Chapters 3 and 5, respectively.)

◆ *Ability to think clearly under stress:* During the salary-review session, you will no doubt experience stress, so you must be able to think under pressure.

◆ *Good listening habits:* You should be capable of responding to questions with logical replies. This requires an ability to listen carefully and attentively.

◆ *Good verbal skills:* You must be able to express your requirements clearly and effectively in speech and in writing.

◆ *Ability to gain respect* from your supervisor and anyone else in the organization This is an essential quality for a manager and should be reflected in your role as a negotiator.

◆ *Empathy:* Sensitivity to the feelings of others will help you to establish and maintain good rapport with your supervisor.

◆ *Personal integrity:* You should represent yourself without exaggeration and without distortion of facts.

Finally, there are certain personality traits that are linked with exceptional managerial skills. To evaluate your own personality, ask yourself the questions in the following list.

If you answer yes to most of these questions, you probably deserve that substantial raise. Go for it—don't settle for an average amount or for an "automatic" increase that reflects just time on the job rather than outstanding performance as a manager.

WHAT IS YOUR WORTH AS A MANAGER?

1. Do you schedule meetings only when necessary?

2. Do you plan an agenda in advance of a meeting?

3. Do you create business or technical plans to guide yourself and your staff?

4. Are you flexible enough to accept changes for meeting the needs of the company?

5. Do you sufficiently analyze the impact of changes?

6. Do you organize your records for easy location?

7. Does your staff receive information on time?

8. Do you put information in writing to your staff or to your supervisors instead of relying on verbal communication?

9. Do you make use of meetings most effectively?

10. Are you responsive to requested information?

11. Are you calm in meeting any crisis?

12. Do you address more than one problem at a time?

13. Do you use time-saving computer techniques?

14. Do you address imperative problems on a timely basis?

15. Do you meet schedules or advise where schedule changes must be made to meet action items?

16. Do you keep morale on the high side?

17. Do you understand your responsibilities?

18. Do you know how to delegate responsibility?

19. Do you show genuine interest in people?

20. Do you remain calm and rational when things don't go your way?

Chapter 2

Recognizing Limitations:

You Versus Your Supervisor

"We judge ourselves by what we feel capable of doing, while others judge us by what we have already done."

—Henry W. Longfellow

You've decided to ask for a raise, and you've gained some idea of negotiation techniques and the personal qualities needed to negotiate effectively. Now, since this isn't a case of the sky's the limit, you should consider the practical limitations on what you can reasonably expect to achieve. This chapter covers some topics associated with these limitations: identifying factors that determine compensation, examining your needs and wants, establishing an acceptable salary range, and analyzing your supervisor's position and personality.

PRINCIPLE 2

Know your adversary.

1. CEO Salaries

Let's start with a review of CEO compensation, consisting of three major parts: salary, bonus, and stock options, and sample a few of the top-paid executives of major national corporations. A representative sample of six top executives has been selected and listed by both total salary and the worth of stock options based on 1996 stock prices.

SOME EXAMPLES OF TOP-PAID EXECUTIVES

For Fiscal Year 1995

	Salary	Bonus	Stock Options	Total
G.H. Lofberg, Pres. Merck & Co. Subsid.	$324,040	365,000	7,431,406	8,120,446
Thomas Gossage, Chmn. Hercules, Inc.	837,508	1,020M	5,560,578	7,418,086
Frank Cahouet, Chmn. Mellon Bank	860,000	645,000	5,330,039	6,835,039
George A. Lorch, Chmn. Armstrong World Ind.	587,500	929,425	3,966,235	5,483,160
John R. Stafford, Chmn. Amer. Home Prod.	1,185M	1,185M	2,237,535	4,937,535
Edgar Woolard, Jr., Chmn. DuPont	1,000M	1,700M	1,809,249	4,509,249

Based on 1996 Stock Prices,
Value of Selected CEOs' Stock Options:

Thomas Gossage, Hercules	$26,306,504
John R. Stafford, Amer Home Prod.	17,535,938
Edgar Woolard, Jr., DuPont	17,479,689
Raymond Smith, Bell Atlantic	6,712,500
Thomas O'Brien, PNC Bank	6,699,269
Drew Lewis, Union Pacific	5,728,362

(Source: Data excerpted from the *Philadelphia Inquirer*, July 1996.)

By any measurement, CEOs' worth seems to be somewhat independent of their performance. Several *Fortune* magazine studies over recent years have identified six factors that determine what CEOs and other top managers are paid.

Performance: A 10 percent improvement in performance can result in a raise of 25 to 30 percent.

Location: Working in New York City, where the cost of living is high, may mean 10 to 35 percent more in pay. (Refer to Chapter 11.)

Business risk: A rise in business risk of 10 percent may result in a 5 percent increase in pay.

Size: The size of a company includes a combination of sales volume, assets, and shareholders' equity. A 10 percent increase in size may raise a CEO's salary by 2 percent.

Industry: CEOs of power utilities are paid the least, followed by CEOs of transportation and retailing concerns.

Tenure: As a rule, a CEO of long standing earns less than a newly hired one. A CEO's salary may decrease by 6 percent for every 5 additional years with the same company.

Even though you're not yet a CEO, the preceding information may be helpful in that the same six factors may also influence a manager's salary.

2. Examining Your Needs and Wants Before a Salary Review

When you request a raise, your supervisor's initial response may be, "Why do you think you deserve an increase?" For this reason, prime prerequisites of a salary review meeting include adequate preparation and job performance above expected levels. When challenged, be specific in stating how you've exceeded expectations. Be ready to list your accomplishments, to explain their benefit to the company, and to describe what you see as your role in the firm, both for the present and in the future.

To start, perform a self-appraisal by answering the following questions:

◆ Are you doing just your job, or more than is expected of you?

◆ Do you fit into the company's long-range plans, and are you promotable?

◆ What are your salary goals—now, a year from now, and in the next decade?

◆ Are you keeping up with your professional education?

◆ What are your performance goals and objectives—now and for the future?

◆ What are your strengths and weaknesses? (Do your strengths outweigh your weaknesses?)

◆ Will you seek employment elsewhere if you are denied a raise that is satisfactory to you?

◆ What can you do to improve your value to your firm?

3. Establishing a Range for Your Increase

Having gained a rough idea of the raise you want, give yourself latitude to negotiate the exact amount. Be prepared with a salary range that you consider acceptable. Your top figure may be higher than the one that has been established by the company for your position (see Chapter 4). Even so, your salary requirements should be based on how important your work is to both your supervisor and the company, and the company's apparent willingness to pay for it.

If you are aware of the company's range, you may want to take the initiative and present your salary requirement first. However, if you are uncertain of the range, let your supervisor, not you, make the initial offer. But before making a counteroffer, question the range: When was it last increased, and when will it be updated? Don't be surprised if your supervisor is reluctant to give you answers. Expect to hear some objections, such as "Company budgets are limited," "Other employees in your category are not making as much as you are now," and "This offer is a lot more than you are currently earning." If this happens, try using closing techniques (see Chapter 7), but first determine the reason(s) that your request is meeting resistance.

4. Understanding Your Supervisor's Viewpoint

When negotiating raises, you and your supervisor are, frankly speaking, adversaries. You want the highest raise you can get. Your supervisor wants to retain a productive and loyal worker at the lowest cost. His or her overall goal is to increase the workload while minimizing the number of employees, and to have these employees follow orders with a minimum number of questions and little need for direction and training. In addition, your supervisor wants to make an impression on his or her own superiors—to demonstrate outstanding performance as a leader, while reducing the number of problems being brought to the attention of upper management. How much your supervisor may be willing to give in return for your assistance in achieving company goals may depend on how well you've "sold" your worth, what you are willing to accept, and what compromises you both are willing to make. How easily you reach an agreement may depend on your replies to questions and how well you keep the salary discussion open until your objective is met.

An important factor with a direct impact on the negotiations is personalities—yours and your supervisor's. You should know how to recognize a person's social style and be aware of the different ways people interact. This knowledge can be useful in winning the other party's respect and acquiring the capability to anticipate his or her remarks and actions. The following are four common personality types:

◆ *Ambitious* types are oriented more toward achieving results than toward dealing with people. They appear uncommunicative and stable, and act independently and competitively in relationships with others. Most people who fall within this category have pleasant, even charming, personalities. However, they tend to slight other people, mainly through failure to recognize good work.

◆ *Extroverts* appear to be communicative, warm, and approachable, but they are also competitive. They may seem to seek your friendship but actually may only want you to follow and support their ambitions. Your relationship with an extrovert may continue only until he or she reaches a self-serving goal.

◆ *Friendly* types are the most people oriented of the personality styles. They treat people as individuals rather than as a means of achieving results or influence. They look for—and usually get—supportive opinions. They are friendly and warm, but they avoid taking risks.

◆ *Introverts* are uncommunicative, levelheaded, and independent. They may show cooperativeness, but are cautious in displaying friendliness and are mainly concerned with getting things done without any personal involvement.

In speaking with your supervisor, you must avoid conflicts caused by differences between each of your personalities. Knowledge of your own personality type helps you to be more diplomatic when dealing with the supervisor.

When meeting with your supervisor to review salary, it's vital that you have a positive attitude. The following list of negative personality types describes behavior and attitudes you should avoid.

◆ *Silent* is unresponsive and withdrawn, and neglects to ask questions to get facts in a meeting with others.

◆ *Concurrent* agrees with everything because he or she has a dire need to be liked and hates to pursue a difference in opinion. Also, he or she is overly concerned with the personal feelings of others.

◆ *Mr. or Ms. Negative* believes that nothing ever works out and usually never takes the advice of others.

◆ *The Bitcher* may complain about the workload and working conditions. He or she may uncover real problems but may present them negatively, which turns people off.

◆ *The Wise Guy* can be the most difficult to get along with. Wise Guys think they know more than any other person. Usually, they are superior in knowledge and performance, but their attitudes rub people the wrong way.

◆ *Low Tolerance Level* types lose their cool very quickly and are most irritating. They are looked upon as losers.

Chapter 3

What Is Your Worth?

"I like thinking big. I always have. To me it's very simple: if you're going to be thinking anyway, you might as well think big."

—Donald Trump
The Art of the Deal

In this part of the book (Chapters 3 to 6), the focus is on prenegotiation strategy: assessing your worth in the current job market and to your company; examining job evaluation, salary administration, and performance appraisal as practiced by the company; taking certain specific steps to prepare for the salary review meeting; and predicting the negotiation tactics that your supervisor may use and planning how to meet them.

Hints for researching salary information are provided in this chapter, and various types of alternatives to raises, better known as options and perks, are described.

PRINCIPLE 3

Job relevancy is important, but personal achievement is better.

1. Your Worth on the Open Market

Before negotiating for a salary increase, it is important to learn what your skills and abilities as a manager are worth in the open market, as well as to your company. One of the best ways to obtain this information is by exchanging salary information with others in similar positions, within and outside the company. Sometimes these peers may not be willing to reveal their own salaries but may volunteer information about the salaries of others. Personnel recruitment agencies are also a good source for determining salary levels as equated to years of experience. Also, many trade periodicals run surveys of salaries. The Bureau of Labor Statistics and even want ads are other good sources of information.

A survey conducted by *Compensation and Benefits Review* among 35 personnel managers and 234 middle managers from the same industry resulted in different opinions about salary raises. Responses from the personnel managers indicated the use of criteria based on factors other than performance. Middle managers, however, preferred pay raises based on performance and were dissatisfied with salary inequities. As a result of the survey, it was concluded that a rewards system for middle managers should be more equitable and incentives given to improve and recognize performance. Another conclusion was that improved managerial performance may help to improve a company's position in relation to the competition.

Now let's look specifically at your market value. A little research on your part will be helpful as a beginning. Your local library may have one or more of the following publications available:

◆ *The Occupational Outlook Handbook*, published by the United States Government Printing Office, describes tomorrow's jobs and comments on each with respect to the type of work, location of employment, training requirements, qualifications, advancement, current and future opportunities, and earnings.

◆ *American Almanac of Jobs and Salaries.*

◆ *National Survey of Professional, Administrative, Technical, and Clerical Pay*, published by the Bureau of Labor Statistics.

◆ *The Encyclopedia of Associations*, issued by Gale Research, lists 18,000 professional organizations.

◆ Trade journals or magazines. (A letter or phone call to a publication may produce pertinent information.)

See Chapter 4 for information regarding salary administration techniques and their effect on your salary and potential raises.

Now ask yourself: How do I fit within the company or organization? When first entering your chosen industry you took a position with the company and either negotiated a salary or accepted what was offered. As you've gained experience in the organization and become more valuable, you've expected periodic salary increases. Your compensation may include several components, such as bonuses, stock options, and other perks. Most industries pay the going rate for your position as you climb up the ladder. However, your value is also determined by how much employees with similar experience earn, what similar positions are paid in other companies in the industry, and the associated law of supply and demand.

2. Your Worth to the Company as a Manager

In Chapter 1, a self-rating test was introduced to explore twenty key factors that may help you evaluate your worth as a manager. The more "yes's" checked off, the more managerial capability you have. But, if you've checked a lot of "no's," the time may be ripe for improving your areas of weakness. Try the test several times and provide honest evaluations. This may be to your advantage. No one will be looking over your shoulder; keep the results private and under your control.

A manager's worth may be considered in terms of performance, peer acceptance, company politics, presentation of self, ability to resolve administrative problems, and skill at handling the pressures of the job. Level of performance may be indicated by how well critical problems are analyzed and solved, whether the manager does more than the job requires, and whether he or she is cooperative, accepts criticism well, and displays motivation. Let's look into some relevant factors.

Accepting responsibility: Failure cannot always be blamed on someone else or attributed to bad luck. When resources and personnel are provided to perform certain functions for a company, a manager must accept responsibility for both good or bad happenings. Mistakes do occur, but a manager should be able to analyze the causes and know how to institute corrective action for present and future problems.

Motivation: A manager may have knowledge, abilities, and skills but lack the motivation to produce. A department with an unmotivated manager is likely to show minimal results.

Self-knowledge: A manager must know his or her strengths and weaknesses. It is important to avoid trying to be what one is not. At the same time a manager must be willing to investigate and apply methods for improving traits and skills that are important for effective performance on the job.

Self-acceptance and acceptance of others: Self-acceptance should not lead to complacency; rather, it means recognizing one's limitations in making improvements. In regard to others, a manager should be sensitive to the needs of fellow managers, subordinates, and superiors. A manager should know how to criticize constructively and should also be able to accept criticism without animosity.

3. How Can I Improve Myself and My Net Worth?

First, let's start thinking about becoming successful and avoiding failure. Minimize your mistakes by keeping a journal of *work input* versus *work output* with appropriate dates (i.e., log in receiving dates, due dates, and dates completed). Schedule your workload, allowing enough time for meetings. Include the name of your staff member who has been assigned the work, but make certain the action required is clearly understood.

Second, set up team meetings for interfacing work assignments and for airing gripes. Encourage openness. Listen and share the concerns of your staff. Remember, how well your staff and you personally perform is a reflection of your capability.

Third, make allies, not adversaries, of your colleagues, by improving the exchange of information. However, avoid too much camaraderie; after all, these associates may also be competing for that more-than-average raise.

Fourth, avoid complacency in your workplace. Work to improve your self-confidence, self-worth, and self-esteem. Feeling secure on your job is *your* responsibility. Thus, never cease educating yourself and keeping your skills up-to-date. Specialization was desirable in the past, but, as a manager, broadening your skills makes you even more desirable. Spend time with those who are one step up from you and your peers.

Make yourself a better leader by assuming more risks, but make sure you can handle them. Rely on your staff to provide experience, additional skills, and brainpower, and learn from them so that your deficiencies will be minimized. Reward your staff with raises—provided, of course, they are well deserved. Show compassion and understanding of their personal problems. Keep your staff informed of the quality of their job performance by using adequate feedback.

4. The Question of Fringe Benefits

When negotiating a raise, a good time to discuss fringe benefits or perks is after you have obtained the highest possible salary increase. Then focus your negotiating skills on getting an improved package of fringe benefits. Remember that benefits come in two primary categories: *fixed* benefits that usually apply to all employees (e.g., health and pension plans), and *flexible* benefits that depend on job classification and may include tangibles such as a larger office with better furniture (and that prestigious carpeting!), free medical examinations, extra insurance coverage, relocation expenses, low-interest loans, flexible hours, a company car (for business and sometimes also for personal use), stock options (e.g., the right to purchase company stock at reduced market values), free legal and financial counseling, membership dues for professional associations and consumer price clubs, extra vacation or free time, a savings plan whereby the company may match part of the employee's savings, and a personal computer that may be kept at home or used while traveling.

Most employees look forward to annual or semiannual raises as a measure of their performance and worth to the firm. But salary increases have decreased in this decade, from 5.57 percent per annum in 1990 to 4.1 percent in 1996. Consequently, management employees and their employers have included the use of incentives to supplement salary increases. Profit sharing, among other benefits, has become most prevalent. The belief is that profit sharing can increase employee productivity and efficiency, and thus company profits.

Even at a junior level, a company benefit plan can add between 20 to 30 percent to one's salary. When considering total salary, you must include benefits such as paid vacations, health, disability and life insurance, stock options, profit sharing, and retirement programs. Interestingly enough, the cost of benefits to a corporation has increased more significantly than basic salaries. If you are advised that raises are limited, some benefits, as described below, may be considered when negotiating a raise:

◆ a bonus, or a larger one

◆ additional vacation days or special days off, such as for your birthday or extra holidays

◆ attendance at workshops, conferences, exhibitions, and seminars that are germane to your field

◆ company-paid professional dues and subscriptions to trade magazines/newsletters.

Bonuses are normally awarded for individual and company performance and overall profitability. Most bonus programs are on an annual basis, but some are for longer durations. The higher you rank in the firm, the more of a probable bonus. Stock options provide a means for employees to invest in the company, making the employee feel more committed. These may be offered at a price lower than the day's trading price and may be cashed in but restricted to a limited number of shares turned in by the duration for which they were held.

Medical insurance costs have become a burden for only one side to handle. Therefore it has become common for both the employee and employer to share the premiums. The choice of health care providers is left to the employee; many select an HMO to keep the cost of premiums more reasonable. A number of companies offer life and disability insurances without cost to the employee but only up to a certain value; above that the employee picks up the additional tab. Retirement plans may consist of two parts: the company-sponsored part wherein only the company contributes, and a 401(k) plan that allows the employee to contribute funds that are tax deferrable until the individual draws a pension after retirement. The first part of the plan requires an employee to endure a waiting period before being vested and entitled to the funds contributed by the company.

Upon reaching the level of middle management, additional benefits and perks may be either offered or negotiated. These are briefly described in the following list.

◆ Interest-free loans, which may cover the purchase of a house.

◆ Bonuses for accepting positions at higher levels of the company.

◆ Spousal-assistance benefits for company transferees, whereby a company finds a spouse a job in the new location or provides retraining.

◆ Health-club membership, as a corporate member or under a company-paid sponsorship.

◆ Financial planning assistance.

◆ A "golden parachute" in the event of future layoff.

Other types of supplements or alternatives to salary increases may include:

◆ Commissions and bonuses, such as higher commissions on sales above a set quota, profit sharing, or performance bonuses.

◆ Cars and expense accounts. A company car can be worth thousands since the company pays for insurance and maintenance.

Expense accounts are usual for sales personnel.

◆ Professional dues and reimbursement for expenses incurred for meetings.

◆ Time off for meetings or for training sessions.

◆ Additional vacation and personal days.

◆ Extra payment for time worked, including holiday premiums, overtime, and shift differentials.

◆ Payments for time not worked, such as holidays, jury duty, medical leave, sick leave, personal days, and vacation days.

◆ Various employee services, including a low-cost cafeteria, athletic team sponsorship, a company store, school-tuition reimbursement, and free work clothes.

◆ Increased financial benefits, such as company contributions toward insurance, stock-purchase plans, and pensions.

Chapter 4

Salary Administration and Compensation

"There is no success without hardship."

—Socrates

During your negotiation for a raise, your supervisor may frequently refer to "company policy about salaries." Since salary administration will certainly affect the outcome of the negotiation, this chapter deals with the topic in detail so that you can include this important element in your planning.

It is no surprise that organizations assign salaries according to the difficulty and importance of job categories. Compensation for these job-related factors usually falls into two categories: (1) equal pay for equal work, and (2) more pay for jobs requiring more responsibilities.

To assist companies in the determination of salaries, job-evaluation methods are established by salary administrators of human resources departments. These administrators, with the assistance of members of management, often compare jobs via various formal and systematic procedures to determine the relative positions of jobs to each other and to salary levels. The basis of any technique utilized is to consider each job in terms of its relative importance to the firm. Furthermore, any chosen method ranks jobs and compares factors involved in performance, such as skills, education, and experience, as well as responsibilities. This is followed by an appraisal system to rate employees and to assist management in salary reviews.

PRINCIPLE 4

Job evaluations and appraisals may measure managerial performance, but without adequate raises they are meaningless.

The objectives of a job-evaluation and performance-appraisal system include:

◆ Providing workable wage structures in a systematic way.

◆ Setting up rates for new or revised job classifications.

◆ Providing a means to compare wage and salary rates within departmental groupings.

◆ Providing a base against which individual performance can be measured.

◆ Providing incentives for employees to strive for higher-level positions.

◆ Providing data to assist management by listing requirements for training, transfers, and promotions.

The amount of a particular raise may be selected from within preestablished salary ranges and may depend greatly on future business plans (or projected revenues). A company may decide to improve its salary levels in order to acquire managers who are considered the "cream of the crop" in the labor market. The company may expect to obtain or retain better leadership by paying more than its competitors. However, the reality of corporate economics may force a company to pay employees the minimum and dilute their responsibilities. In this case, upward adjustment of wage levels may occur only in response to excessive labor turnover and absenteeism.

To help determine salaries, companies may refer to information on labor markets and review current economic conditions, recent union settlements, and future prospective revenues. A factor of lesser importance may be cost-of-living standards versus community location.

1. Job Standards and Salary Administration

For skilled workers the salary ranges and wage increases established will depend on the types of workers to be recruited, differentials between labor categories, and employee demands. The number of steps within a range and its bandwidth (i.e., low to high value) will depend on the period of time allowed for an employee to achieve proficiency in the skills required for the job.

Determining a manager's market value may be more difficult since job requirements may not be as well defined as those for lower-echelon positions. Professionals often have staff positions, and many in-line managers believe that they function like professionals. Since the work of a professional involves tasks few others can perform, evaluation (by the company) of a professional can be most difficult. Duties may be identified by employing generic job descriptions. Maturity curves, which show age (usually in terms of years since receiving the first degree) versus monthly salary, may be used in addition to job-evaluation or performance-appraisal methods to provide recognition to those with more years of excellence and proven loyalty. (See next page for a typical maturity curve.)

Salary levels often depend on salary surveys of an overall industry; here, the basis of compensation is the job market. Also, salaries of managers may be influenced by the relationship of their pay to that of their subordinates. Professional organizations can provide salary information obtained from surveys that may be categorized by age, years of experience since attainment of a degree, and rated job performance. In some cases private salary surveys, conducted by a company or a consulting firm, may be required to determine regional versus global salary differences.

As stated above, job evaluation (or standards) relates all job categories in a company to each other and provides wage scales. This rational but complex system of compensation requires administrators with good judgment skills. A job-evaluation system is concerned primarily with job categories and secondarily with the people who fill the positions in these categories.

Creating job standards may involve the following steps:

◆ Conducting a job study or analysis of required work output.

◆ Deciding on the criteria that make one job more valuable than another to management.

A Typical Maturity Curve

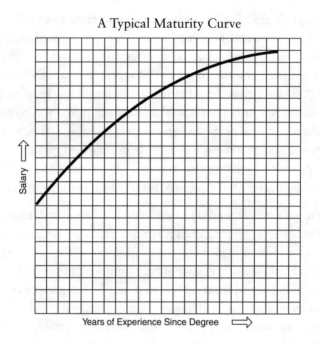

◆ Choosing a job-evaluation system that correlates jobs.

◆ Using a committee (drawn from management) to review and approve a program and to price each job level.

A common method of salary structuring is based on a point-factor system. Each occupation is rated according to established factors. Each factor is weighted and assigned a number of points. Then the points are totaled to determine a point score for each job category. Once jobs are rated, pay scales are assigned. Salary levels within each category are correlated to a formula that links points and pay levels.

Typically, job factors may include:

1. Knowledge and skills (including experience and internal and external relationships and dexterity)   60–280 points

2. Mental demands (or physical effort)   8–140

3. Accountability (responsibilities: in-line supervisory or staff advisory)   11–160

4. Working conditions (hazards, location, etc.)   0–20

As would be expected, the higher the point total, the more a job is worth.

2. Performance Appraisals

Perhaps your company employs a performance-rating system that evaluates an employee's performance and can influence the size of a raise. The system may include a performance appraisal that is initiated by the supervisor, reviewed by both the employee and the supervisor, emended to resolve disagreements, and signed by both parties before its submittal to the human resources department. A performance appraisal, which excludes any discussion of raises, precedes a merit review, the latter depending on results of the appraisal. The appraisal may be designed to highlight your assets and liabilities. Perhaps you may gain time to improve your deficiencies and to demonstrate superior performance; then, at the salary review meeting, the improvements may influence the size of the raise you can negotiate.

Implementing a "pay for performance" standard is difficult. Although annual or periodic raises may be expected, top managers will be rewarded with better than normal raises if the company considers them valuable and not expendable in case of downsizing and layoffs. The employee with written evidence of outstanding performance is in a better position for now and the future. He or she should make sure that the supervisor is apprised of this. A monthly progress report, whether required as a company policy or not, is highly recommended.

Watch out for the company that hires persons with equal skills to yours but pays them higher salaries or bonuses as new recruits. Be careful in obtaining information about these people, especially if the company considers disclosures about salary and personnel as proprietary. Having this knowledge could lead to dismissal. Also, be prepared to face the company that prefers to hire personnel with fewer years of experience than you if it may be contemplating laying off the higher paid employee and using the new employee as a replacement. In this case, worrying about a raise becomes secondary. Instead, either concentrate on resigning from the company and finding a new employer (refer to Chapter 11) or finding another job while waiting for the other shoe to drop. Any action you take must be carefully planned. Use a checklist by dividing a paper into three columns: benefit, yes, and no. For every fact you notate about leaving, check off a yes or no. If there are more checks in the yes column than in the no column, it's time to seek new employment. If the opposite is true, bite the bullet and stay where you are.

Both the performance appraisal and the merit review should be conducted on a regular basis. If they fall behind schedule, this is cause for concern; any delinquency can affect your salary adversely since all future increases are based on percentages of your current salary. With the effects compounded over a number of years, continual late reviews will be reflected in a salary lower than you deserve.

3. Results of a Survey of Managers' Compensation

In a survey conducted by the author, directors and managers of human resources departments were asked for their opinions, as salary administrators, on the importance of six factors in determining raises for managers of their organizations. The personnel queried included representatives from both large and small firms. As might be anticipated, they unanimously ranked performance on the job as the top factor. The others—seniority/tenure, outside market value, size of firm, location of firm, and profitability of firm—received inconsistent rankings. The administrators were also asked to name any other factor(s) that they thought should be considered. The gamut ran from the individual (skill) needs of a firm—education and specialty—to compensating for inequities within salary levels. In reply to a question regarding the most influential factor in granting a manager a higher than average raise, the answer was again unanimous: outstanding performance!

Most companies in the survey preferred to adapt maturity curves or other industrial-standard methods for determining salary structures or to create custom-made point-factor systems or to establish their own systems for market comparisons and employee appraisals. However, whatever systems were employed, the companies considered them proprietary and would not reveal details.

More recently, computer software has been developed to provide standard methods for employee performance reviews. Two programs, "Performance Now" and "Review Writer," simplify the review and are described in the Appendix.

Although few organizations recognize age or seniority as contributors to experience, most pay ranges involve some movement based on seniority. Higher level jobs seem to be filled with higher seniority people. Maturity curves usually show that salaries level off after approximately 25 years.

Chapter 5

Preparing for Salary Review Meetings

"Firmness in support of fundamentals, with flexibility in tactics and methods, is the key to any hope of progress in negotiation."

—Dwight D. Eisenhower

Your preparation for any salary review meeting should include the following four items:

◆ Establishing and maintaining a personal activity log.

◆ Making yourself aware of relevant salary statistics.

◆ Improving your profitability to the firm, and demonstrating your worth.

◆ Establishing the salary and options that will be acceptable to you.

Let's consider each of these items separately.

PRINCIPLE 5

Plan your moves; then move your plans.

1. Establish and Maintain a Personal Activity Log

It is recommended that you keep an up-to-date job journal, recording significant accomplishments from the first day of your employment with the firm. Record your achievements and ideas for making progress, referring specifically to material in your field. Be sure to include a record of your past raises, with dates and percentages; a graphical presentation may be advantageous. Study your business associates (your supervisor, subordinates, subcontractors, customers), and record anything that may be significant as an indication of their skills versus yours.

Any time you receive a commendation, make sure it is in writing and placed with your activity log. If the human resources department maintains a personnel docket system, request access to it periodically. Retain a file of ways in which you have improved your performance over the current period to the benefit of the firm, including courses taken to improve your skills, accomplishments beyond the routine work tasks, awards received within and outside the company, articles written for trade publications, and professional projects in which you were involved.

In addition, keep your resume current. Your resume states your qualifications, which may sometimes be challenged during a negotiation.

2. Be Aware of Relevant Salary Statistics

As far as possible, familiarize yourself with your company's salary administration policies (see Chapter 4), including the creation of wage levels, frequency of raises, and methods of rating jobs. Research the field of your expertise to determine what other firms are paying managers with similar skills (see Chapter 3). Study survey reports. Place yourself within various salary structures, and determine your worth to the firm and to the outside market.

Refer to Chapter 11 for typical salaries of professional positions and regional effects on salaries.

Regardless of any backlash that may result from downsizing, firms need reward systems to assure loyalty, increase productivity, and facilitate the recruiting of new employees. Studies have indicated that many firms have reward programs for managers based on the corporation's annual profit and that firms recognize the need to emphasize long-term benefits. An award system of longer than a year's duration is also described as a means to encourage improved performance and retain managers for longer periods.

3. Improve Your Profitability to the Firm, and Be Ready to Document It

You demonstrate to your company how necessary and how profitable you are when you make things happen. The actual work may be done by your subordinates, but your administrative abilities—your direction and control—lead to accomplishment and results.

Become an expert in your area of responsibility, so that others will seek you out and recognize you as a reliable source of information. Improve your knowledge of company operations and policies, both within and outside your department. Be recognized as a high achiever by accepting more than your share of work and delivering good results. If given the opportunity or responsibility, hire top-notch subordinates who will earn you respect and credibility as a leader. Be friendly to all personnel on all levels of the company; recognize people as individuals and avoid office politics, which can backfire very badly. You can end up rubbing the right people the wrong way.

In his book *Playing to Win*, Fran Tarkenton approaches the value of an employee to a company in another way. "When people ask me how to get a 'winning attitude,' I tell them there is no such thing as a winning attitude. There is only a *winning performance*." This concept usually starts at the top of an organization and trickles down through the various branches. Unless this description fits the organization in which you are employed, perhaps you had better prospect for a new job elsewhere. Your superiors may be sitting on you, figuratively speaking, and denying you the opportunity to be a self-motivator and to demonstrate outstanding performance.

But let's explore Tarkenton's method. He developed a procedure, using the acronym PRICE, which he claims may provide steps for creating a winning performance:

P = Pinpoint *any measurable performance of yours that needs to be changed.*

R = Record *the performance on a chart for everyone to see.*

I = Identify *the results of the performance: how much money or time is lost as a result of inattention or a job poorly done;* then intervene *to modify the performance*

C = Change *the consequences of that behavior; give reinforcement and performance feedback in the form of praise and recognition.*

E = Evaluate *the changes in job performance; continue to review yourself or your employees and modify the consequences based on the direction of progress.*

How you achieved performance goals since your last raise and what you plan to achieve after you receive your next increase should be considered. Always use specific figures to support any claims of increased productivity, new skills acquired, labor-hours saved, and long-term benefits that you have initiated, such as improved employee morale and new product developments.

How does your compensation differ from the salaries of your subordinates? There should be an ample difference to adequately differentiate management status from lower levels. This difference serves to motivate those reporting to you to set their goals on replacing you as you move up the ladder in the organization. Of course, you may seek increased compensation for subordinates who demonstrate superior performance. In that case the salary gap may shrink and provide you with another reason to request a larger paycheck.

Superior performance merits acknowledgment, by your supervisor and by management, that you are an outstanding manager and an excellent team leader whose efforts help make the firm profitable.

4. Establish Acceptable Salary and Option Limits

How do you establish what you consider acceptable salary limits? In Chapter 3, the subject of job worth was emphasized as a major concern for the raise seeker. Before establishing any limit, you should examine the slope of a maturity curve showing pay distribution to see where you best fit in respect to your position and where you think you should fit relative to your performance. Do you think you are being compensated fairly, on the basis of the pay distribution curve?

In your review, you may discover inequities in your salary as compared with the compensation of fellow managers on the same level. Alternatively, the outside market may be competing for experienced individuals like you. These disclosures may assist you in the negotiation. As stated previously, however, the best weapon is a reasonable salary range and a list of perks (with dollar equivalents) to supplement the salary that you plan to demand.

5. Surviving Downsizing

In a downsizing economy you have little job security, so as previously stated, you should avoid confrontation with your supervisor. Furthermore, you should find out about projects being planned and what positions may suit you or may match your qualifications. Be alert to opportunities and look to where you can move ahead. (Most companies provide job postings for any openings.)

Staying late when necessary or offering to work overtime will show your interest in and dedication to a project. More recognition is possible when you approach your supervisor to discuss work assignments informally. But make sure you've done your homework and are prepared for any questions that may be asked of you.

Recognize your deficiencies in fulfilling current and future roles at work. Perhaps an advanced degree is required or more experience in the industry is needed. Take advantage of educational or seminar programs that may be offered. As emphasized in other chapters, make yourself more valuable. Let your superiors know what your goals are and what you expect of them and the company.

Chapter 6

Predicting Your
Supervisor's Moves

"One man's word is no man's word; we should quietly hear both sides."

—Goethe

Let's come back now to your superior, that adversary figure in the negotiation whose personality and motives were briefly considered in Chapter 2. Here we'll attempt a fuller analysis of what makes this important individual tick, so to speak, and we'll outline a one-to-one strategy for success in your salary negotiation.

Now, either you are aware of your supervisor's traits or you must get to know him or her better. In that respect, you should not enter the raise negotiation "cold"! Watch out for power-game tactics that your supervisor may play, and learn how to play along. Be prepared to accept some criticism, even if it appears abusive, whimsical, or insensitive. Anticipate your supervisor's critical questions ("What have you accomplished lately"?) and statements ("You've only been here for a short time"; "You're at the top of the range now"; "You may be doing excellent work now, but once I give you a raise you'll probably relax"). Some of these arguments may sound familiar to you.

PRINCIPLE 6

You probably won't get everything you ask for, but you can surely try!

1. Getting to Know Your Boss

Your relationship with your supervisors depends, in many ways, on how you view them. You may also wonder how they perceive you, understand you or attempt to understand you. The best way for them to get to know you is if you first understand them.

Many business pressures may be hanging over a boss's head. Your supervisor may have been informed of cost-reduction requirements, a pressure builder that must be passed down the line. He or she may be concerned about applying strategies during the salary review session that, if misunderstood, could backfire. It is essential to recognize that your supervisor is human and subject to the same frailties as you. In short, understand the responsibilities and pressures that he or she may be up against, and try a sympathetic approach. Your supervisor needs to be needed, and the reverse, it is hoped, is also true: you too are needed.

What about your supervisor's background? Have you seen his or her resume, or talked about education, business experience, sports, marital status? Is your supervisor active in professional or civic organizations? Find out what your common interests are, and record them in your activity log book (see Chapter 5).

2. Using Positive Approaches

Many bosses feel that negotiating with an employee should turn out to be a win/lose situation. Your supervisor may also have been trained in negotiation techniques, particularly in methods to get you to agree to what he or she wants you to think is reasonable. Let's look at some positive approaches that you can plan to use in a variety of situations:

◆ Keep your voice calm and well modulated. It's possible your supervisor may be watching whether you seem confident or nervous and may react accordingly. Watch your tone (and volume) of voice.

◆ Avoid confrontation. Preserve camaraderie by sticking to a "win/win" philosophy.

◆ Keep the discussion within your current and future period of employment; avoid being held responsible for mistakes the company made in the past.

◆ When questioned about future performance, ask your supervisor to apprise you of the company's or the department's future plans. Then both of you should discuss how well you fit into these plans.

◆ Keep the discussion lively and relevant; a dull or wandering session can end disastrously without much accomplished. Stick to the subject of your salary needs; don't be sidetracked.

◆ When asked a question, think before you respond; never fear a moment of silence.

3. Playing Along with "Power" Tactics

Be prepared, when reacting to your supervisor, to avoid open resentment or hostility. Let him or her talk! Perhaps your supervisor needs a sympathetic ear or a chance to blow off steam as a result of mounting pressures. Examine the situation for positive movements that may lead you into a "yes, but . . ." routine, in which you basically agree but do not totally acquiesce. If you like what you hear, give an affirmative response, but don't overdo it; few bosses appreciate yes-men or apple polishers.

Some supervisors with weak personalities may apply power tactics in an attempt to conceal insecurities. These people are not as powerful as they pretend they are, but you must play along with them. Never "bad-mouth" your supervisor!

By remaining firm and cool, you show flexibility and poise. You should seriously consider transferring to another department or even leaving the firm, however, if your supervisor stubbornly avoids responding to a request, whether it concerns salary or a promotion. Recognize delaying tactics; if requested to wait for a reasonable period, agree only when promised you will have a definite answer at the end of the waiting time. Always recognize that your supervisor should also expect a promotion or a raise in the immediate future, and be ready to help him or her get that advancement. As your supervisor moves up the corporate ladder, you will find an empty rung above you.

Dr. Tessa Warschaw, in her book *Winning by Negotiation*, identifies "The Power Game—and How to Play It with Each Stylist." Brief descriptions of the various stylists are provided below to assist you in classifying your supervisor. By recognizing the various types she describes, you may better understand how to cope with how your boss wields power.

"Jungle fighters" love power and can be savage and merciless in pursuing their objectives, but can be handled. Avoid being intimidated, and don't let them think you fear them.

"Dictators" must be in control and will treat you as a follower. Avoid being used; but if you cooperate with and stick by them, you can provide valuable support to their egos.

"Silhouettes" are secretive about themselves and their motivations. Thus you may be required to draw upon outside sources for information about them. They may provide opinions but approach things quietly. Don't be afraid of silence, but answer questions directly and fully to hold their attention.

"Big mammas and daddies" control with love and approval and avoid power confrontations. Watch out lest you be treated like a child, for they may want to manipulate you into their way of thinking.

"Soothers" project a message that they need your help, but they don't like to listen to your side of the story. They will deviate from the subject, so you must guide them back on track.

Now let's switch roles and review how your boss may conceive and manage his or her subordinates who may be bothersome. Kare Anderson, in her book *Getting What You Want*, identifies those types who bother you the most and how to handle them:

"Dominators" are aggressive and take over meetings. It's best to avoid escalating conflict in standing up to them. Don't resist them but don't withdraw. Carefully mirror their body language and voice tone. Focus on your goals, overlooking their behavior. If they should lose their temper, allow them to blow off steam.

"Know-It-Alls" need to have their accomplishments acknowledged, and often cite similar accomplishments by others to emphasize their relative importance.

Both of the above types tend to monopolize conversations, which can be most frustrating to the other party.

"Agreeables" should be asked if they understand what you are saying and are not just agreeing with you. Make sure you tell them exactly what you want. Then solicit their ideas on how they wish to proceed.

"Won't Work People" are skeptical. Be cautious in dealing with this type and minimize their contact with the rest of the group. If possible, reduce their responsibilities. Using guidelines of how to work together as a team, you may avoid frustrations of insubordination.

"Bumps on the Log" require having a fire lit under them to get them to participate. Ask them what they expect from the negotia-

tions and clearly explain your goals or objectives. Force their participation by giving them a choice of two alternatives.

"Complainers" think nothing is ever right. Listen to their complaints, acknowledging that you heard them. Afterwards, ask them for recommendations. It's possible you may not want them around anymore and may consider having them dismissed or transferred to another department, even if technically they are outstanding.

4. Anticipating What Your Supervisor May be Willing to Give

As described in Chapter 4, salary administration in a company consists of a formal program that provides management not only with job-evaluation methods but also with data on employee performance and salary statistics. Such a salary administration program defines acceptable performance measurements and attempts to recognize that better performers are entitled to higher pay. Salaries are distributed within certain ranges. The company's policy may include both automatic raises, which are given in steps, and merit raises, which are generally initiated by supervisors. Progression through ranges can be automatic, meritorious, or a combination of both, depending on the employee's skill and experience. Merit raises are based on the idea that wage increases should be earned through increased proficiency or quality of performance and viewed as incentives for future performance. Many managers, however, perceive all raises as identical and regard money in general as an incentive for future performance rather than as a reward for past achievement.

Pay raises within each salary range may be considered to hinge on the individual employee's performance, pay history, current position within the range, experience, time elapsed since the last raise, the amount of that raise, the salaries of others holding similar positions, labor market considerations, and, most important, the company's financial condition.

So what can you expect from your supervisor? Will cost of living and any related salary adjustments be ignored? Will your supervisor blindly follow salary administration techniques or guidelines? Let's face it—your supervisor will prefer to offer you a salary in accordance with the going rate in a competitive market rather than meet what you feel you need for survival in inflationary times.

OK, boss—you've reached the end of your rope, and you've run out of excuses for not providing a better raise. Let's go one step further! How about a promotion and the increase that accompanies it? A promotion certainly would open up a new rate range, as well as provide recognition for outstanding performance. But what about that "no opening for a promotion" response? If you can't get a satisfactory reply, you might plan to ask your supervisor to move you to another area or another department of the company that may provide an opportunity for advancement. But be cautious; avoid a threat to leave the company. An ultimatum may land you in the unemployment office. Nevertheless, your strategy should include a refusal to take a negative response as a final answer!

Chapter 7

Negotiation Strategies and Tactics

"Let us never negotiate out of fear. But let us never fear to negotiate."

—John F. Kennedy inaugural address,
January 20, 1961

The planning stage is over, and the big day is drawing near. It's time to consider the tactics that will result in a successful negotiation.

Because preparation is so important, however, let's first review and summarize some important prenegotiation strategies and tactics.

PRINCIPLE 7

> *To be considered successful, a salary negotiation should leave both parties feeling as though they have won something: you, a satisfactory raise; your supervisor, a contented, productive manager.*

1. Preparation—the Key to Obtaining a Raise

Start with Yourself.

To get the raise you're seeking, you must first establish plans and objectives to improve the areas of your performance that have a direct bearing on company efficiency, revenues, and profit. A solid record of outstanding work may be all that's required, as well as proof of an improving quality of performance. You should document your accomplishments, making sure that your supervisor acknowledges them, before attempting to negotiate a raise. Make sure that you have studied salary standards and have kept an activity log of your performance (see Chapter 5). As stated previously, establish your salary range—your target raise and your bottom-line raise; the latter will prevent you from accepting a less-than-satisfactory raise in the heat of the moment. Consider the most difficult issues that are likely to arise, and prepare alternatives or supplements to salary requirements (i.e., fringe benefits; see Chapter 3). Try predicting what objections your supervisor will raise and how you can overcome them.

Assess Your Supervisor and His or Her Position.

If possible, be aware of some personal details about your supervisor: marital status, spouse's name, ages of children, hobbies, and any job-related interests that parallel yours, for example. Perhaps you can also find out something about his or her track record in awarding raises and promotions. To obtain this information, you may want to invite your supervisor to lunch or get together for an informal chat during or after working hours.

Most people are predictable. If a person does something once, he or she is likely to do it again. What can other people tell you about strategies your supervisor has used in the past? Is there anything on record that can give you clues?

Consider the decision-making hierarchy of your firm. With whom does your supervisor consult on salary administration matters? If he or she isn't authorized to get you a raise, who is?

Review your prior pay increases for frequency and rate. Seek out information about the frequency of increases given to your peers, how the raises compare to yours, the company's financial condition, and your department's current and future budgets.

Be Ready to Respond Effectively to Conflict.

Conflict is a part of life. To get the raise you want, you may have to endure conflict, and you should be prepared for it. During the meeting you may say things your supervisor may not like or doesn't want to hear; therefore, you must expect negative reactions. Negotiating is by nature a stressful task, and the stress increases as the level of difficulty rises.

During a salary negotiation, belligerence and argumentativeness gain you nothing. Questions are much less threatening than statements. Whenever possible, phrase your statements in the form of questions. By remaining calm and courteous, you are more likely to achieve a successful outcome.

Improve Your Listening Skills.

Practice active listening. During the negotiation you shouldn't stop listening to plan what you'll say next, or drift away because you think you know what your supervisor will say. Instead, plan to jot down notes. Probably your supervisor, even if sympathetic to your case, has some points to make. Patiently listen—and don't interrupt! If you don't understand what's being said, say so—and ask specific questions.

Ensure Physical Comfort and an Appropriate Setting.
Here are some points to consider:

◆ Come to the meeting well rested and physically comfortable. Eat sensibly, not gluttonously, before the meeting; and wear clothes and shoes that fit properly.

◆ If you have a choice, sit alongside your supervisor at his or her desk or at the conference table. (Sitting in front of your supervisor's desk or at the opposite side of the table creates the appearance of separation by rank.)

◆ Request that the meeting take place where there won't be any interruptions by other employees or by telephone calls. You will need the supervisor's undivided attention during the negotiation.

◆ Refrain from smoking, even if your supervisor lights up.

2. The Structure of the Negotiation

Most salary negotiations involve an offer-and-counteroffer sequence, which obviously involves bargaining. Bargain well and your earning power will improve. Since we all have a desire to improve our lifestyles, we should use bargaining power all the time. Hence, all of us can gain by improving our negotiating skills.

Expect your supervisor to present an opening offer that is based on company salary administrative policies. Chances are the offer will be lower than what you consider acceptable. Therefore, you must be prepared to present the reasons you think you deserve a bigger raise. This counteroffer should be based on established objectives, such as an estimate of a reasonable range of salary increases and fringe benefits of comparable monetary value. (Chapter 5 contains advice on preparing for the salary review meeting.)

Although your initial position will probably be higher than your supervisor's, it should not be so high that it precludes reaching agreement on a salary acceptable to you. You should be prepared, however, to accept an offer that is less than the high side of your objective, such as a percentage of increase that falls within your established range of acceptance (see Chapter 4).

Bear in mind that your supervisor may be bound by company policy to accept only a counteroffer that falls within his or her authority, even if a higher offer can be reasonably supported. If the company-authorized rate is below the lower end of your range, you will have to start applying your bargaining skills. You must be prepared to show, perhaps by citing your extraordinary performance or comparable higher salaries for the same job, why the numbers must be bumped up.

Written agreements detailing salaries and fringe benefits are the preferred way of summing up salary negotiations. Other terms of employment, such as working conditions, severance pay, advance notification of termination, and so on, are generally covered by law or written company policy. If some of these items are not specified, make sure they are provided in any agreement. (Prior to the negotiation, refresh your memory or check your files. Perhaps you had signed an employment agreement as a new employee. Compare the original with the later agreement for concurrence of items or for conflicting items that may not be beneficial to you.) If the resultant agreement is unsatisfactory—whether it be for raises or other benefits—you may have to weigh staying in your current job against seeking new employment (refer to Chapter 11).

3. Examples of Negotiation Strategies and Tactics

Salary negotiation involves varied techniques that are applied to enable the sessions to proceed amicably, without friction, so that an agreement satisfactory to both sides is readily reached. Experienced negotiators use a variety of means to accomplish their objectives. Knowing when to use a particular strategy requires a sense of timing. Negotiation techniques include both planned strategies and spontaneous or extemporaneous tactics.

Regardless of what transpires during the meeting, an atmosphere of mutual respect between the parties should be maintained at all times, especially if you and your supervisor work in a close relationship and expect to continue to do so over a long period.

Here are four commonly used strategies:

Combinations: To start, you may introduce simultaneously several positive factors in regard to your performance. In this way your supervisor may be forced to consider the broad picture. All points raised should be viewed as equally important. If your supervisor minimizes any of them at the time they are raised, you may wish to repeat some of them later.

Coverage: Some supervisors choose to avoid discussing details. They hope to conduct the meeting with as little time and effort as possible. However, you have a right to slow down the pace to provide adequate time for presenting each meritorious factor separately. After all, you expended considerable effort in preparing for the meeting, and you don't want this to go for nought. Your reasons for getting the raise must be properly addressed. Some supervisors obviously prefer a broad coverage, because if each factor is discussed separately, the rationale for minimizing a raise may be refuted.

Statistics: Each party should be certain that any figures and statistics that are presented are valid. Here again, preparation pays off. For example, if one party argues that certain statistical trends are representative of the future for the occupation in question, the other party should be prepared to reply.

One Step at a Time: Using this effective strategy, you convincingly present one point after another until your objective is reached. (Essentially, this is the antithesis of coverage.) Each meritorious factor is addressed separately to emphasize your assets and value.

The four tactics described below are helpful in reaching an agreement:

Patience: This tactic involves delaying, suspending, or postponing an answer at the moment to give one party a chance to think over the other's proposition. However, the other side also has the same opportunity and may change his or her offer after further consideration. Any counteroffer should be withheld until it is felt that the other party will seriously reconsider the original proposition. This tactic is often useful when a supervisor responds to your demands with a statement such as "You've got to be kidding!"

Timing: The ideal time for initiating discussions about a raise may be when your supervisor comes into your office for a chat. However, you should keep this exchange informal; use it to set up a formal meeting at a later date that allows you adequate time for preparation.

Surprise: This requires a sudden shift in position. For example, you may request that your supervisor call in an immediate superior when an obstacle to reaching a salary agreement creates an impasse. Once the superior is included in the session, major factors should be reiterated and emphasized in the hope that the new negotiator is more reasonable and that a satisfactory agreement can be reached. However, this tactic is recommended only as a last resort, since it may offend your supervisor.

Diversion: This tactic calls for one party to exaggerate the information under discussion. Because this can be construed as a bluff, you should be cautious and avoid unfounded claims. Your supervisor is using the diversion tactic when he or she makes questionable promises about future raises in the hope that you will withdraw or reduce your present demands.

4. Closing Techniques

What do you do when you've tried applying salary negotiation techniques but have failed to reach even a satisfactory compromise? How about trying closing techniques? Many sales personnel have certainly found them to be effective.

Some people possess proficiency in applying both negotiating and closing techniques. If you are among these lucky ones, you are blessed with powerful tools, but you must use them cautiously. You must be tactful to avoid upsetting your supervisor and to prevent him or her from becoming disenchanted with a loyal and productive manager. In particular, you need to avoid the possibility of being discharged.

Closing techniques are usually associated with sales but may be considered to be related to negotiating techniques in that both result in either "acceptance" or "rejection." In closing, however, rejection, which may mean that you have not been convincing enough to support your claim, is final; whereas, in negotiating, rejection may occur until agreement or a compromise is reached. Regardless of the techniques employed, your supervisor is likely to agree to a particular raise only when convinced that it is both reasonable and justifiable.

To clarify the primary *difference*, we may define *closing* as a technique employed by a seller (or, in our case, the seeker of a raise), whereas *negotiating* is used jointly by both a seller (you) and a buyer (in our case, your supervisor). Commonality between the two is most prevalent when sessions are deadlocked. In such cases the negotiation tactics ordinarily employed may very well be supplemented by closing techniques.

Closing, like negotiating, is an art requiring knowledge and skill, and is developed primarily through experience. It takes skill to read "ready-to-buy" signs and to overcome objections, as well as dexterity in applying negotiating techniques. Also, as a seeker your mental attitude should always be positive; you should be persistent but remain calm, alert, and ready for any element of surprise. To a certain degree, the closing technique requires acting ability—when it is time to be cordial, you perform accordingly; when it is time to be firm and dynamic, you rise dramatically to the occasion. You must know when to apply the appropriate tactic. You must sense when to talk (to ask questions) and when to shut your mouth (especially when you've reached the end of the line—your preplanned limitations). Your approach must suggest self-confidence; conceal any fear of failure.

If your supervisor seems unimpressed by your presentation, you should not get discouraged but should think in terms of "I failed to make him or her understand." Dust yourself off and *try again*! A common tactic is to use a positive "Yes, but . . ." approach. This leads the other party to think mistakenly that agreement has been reached and to relax his or her guard, offering you the opportunity to advance new arguments or emphasize old ones. Another tactic is to ask "Why?" in response to any item of disagreement. But make sure you keep quiet and listen to the answer!

Remember that the principle in handling objections is never to argue back. Simply reiterate: go over the same tracks, but use new arguments and clearer explanations. The temptation to retaliate in a hostile way is always present and becomes greater as the negotiation drags on. You may win a particular argument; but in so doing, you may also antagonize your supervisor so that an agreement is less likely to be achieved.

5. Compromise—the Key to Reaching Agreement

In most cases, agreements result from compromises. The negotiation process requires both parties to aim toward achieving a settlement, and a compromise may be the only means of reaching agreement. In approaching a compromise, each party should attempt to summarize the other's position, pointing out specific areas of difference and presenting facts or opinions that support each position.

Some Aspects of Compromise.

Commonly, each side establishes its "last" position before being willing to compromise. In the raise negotiation, two possible bases of agreement should be considered: a total raise now or progressive increases.

Two types of compromise are possible:

◆ Both sides feel a degree of satisfaction: an agreement has been reached for an acceptable "best" raise.

◆ One side is satisfied but not the other: because one party is stronger, an unbalanced compromise has been reached.

Tactical Mistakes to Avoid in Reaching an Agreement.

To negotiate successfully, you should avoid the following mistakes:

Unreasonable opening demands: By aiming high, you give yourself room to negotiate. However, your opening demands should not be so unrealistic that your supervisor either postpones meeting with you or refuses to listen to what you have to say.

Free concessions: Never make a concession without getting one in return. Unconditioned concessions frequently turn into freebies for which your supervisor generally will not reciprocate.

Rapid negotiations: Rapid settlements are frequently extreme win/lose deals. The less prepared and the less skilled negotiator is often victimized by his or her opponent. Put yourself in command; slow things down.

Settling too quickly: Agreeing too quickly incurs a greater chance of not reaching or even nearing your objective. Be ready to "sleep on it," particularly if you have any doubts about accepting the raise offered. Resist any pressure for acceptance. Good deals are almost never bargained quickly.

Negotiating when surprised: Don't bargain unless you're fully prepared! If something unforeseen comes up, take a break. Ask your supervisor for time to review the proposition.

Fear of Silence: If you keep your mouth shut and show that you're listening, your supervisor may reciprocate. After you have asked a question or if you're in the process of thinking, keep quiet. Don't be embarrassed about long silences.

Getting angry: Keeping cool is a great advantage. Never lose your temper (at least, not obviously). Remember: You will probably continue to work with your supervisor after this review session. Also, emotion hampers the ability to think clearly. If you respond negatively to your supervisor, you may forget your prepared strategy and hence lose the "game"!

Failure to Get the Agreement in Writing: It is not enough just to reach an agreement; you need to get a written record. A handshake is fine, but ask your supervisor to put the agreed-to rate and perks in writing to avoid a lapse of memory. But be tactful in requesting the written agreement.

Negotiating when fatigued: Tired negotiators often make foolish errors and may be easily influenced by their opponents. For this reason be sure to get enough sleep the night before the meeting. Also, avoid drinking or smoking immediately before and while negotiating.

Letting your guard down: A few moments of carelessness can destroy the results of a hitherto-successful session. Your supervisor may have been waiting for his or her chance to take advantage of you. Don't relax until an agreement has been reached.

Unduly prolonging the negotiation: In negotiating, as in playing poker, there's a time to hold and a time to fold. If you push too far, your irritated supervisor may react by calling off the meeting or even taking a more drastic step, such as getting rid of you.

Unethical Behavior.

Negotiations can be abused by using misleading statements to exaggerate your worth and capability. Unethical behavior may involve promoting yourself against those vying for the same or like positions or salary advancements, or for getting a better raise than you deserve. If you are caught bending the truth, it could lead to the company taking disastrous action against you, from holding back a raise or promotion to dismissal.

6. Mistakes in Dealing with Company Policies

As you gain experience and develop salary negotiating skills, you may observe many personnel mistakenly accepting misconceptions as fact. For example, employees may be led to believe that in large corporations salaries are established by policy and are not negotiable. Salary ranges may have been established to be competitive to similar positions in other companies and can be quite broad. The midpoint of the range is probably the salary awarded to the capable worker who has experience in his or her field. But the spread is most likely plus and minus 20 percent of that midpoint. Therefore, the company may have more money to negotiate than they want you to realize. Nevertheless, be careful and don't negotiate unless you understand fully the components of the compensation package and what your skills are worth on the market. By being stubborn, you may alienate your supervisor rather than succeed in extracting other benefits. Smaller companies may not have established salary policies but are willing to pay more for the more skilled worker.

Other mistakes may include:

◆ Failure to obtain a better starting salary, which in turn may limit raises in the future.

◆ Attempting to improve your odds of getting a job by accepting a lower starting salary. As mentioned, this can backfire down the road.

◆ Shying away from negotiating a raise by naively believing the company automatically recognizes good performance and provides raises in return.

SUMMARY: IMPORTANT ITEMS TO REMEMBER ABOUT NEGOTIATING:

Here are some guidelines to keep in mind:

Failure to agree may be attributed to:

◆ Failure to provide adequate supporting arguments.

◆ A poor mental attitude.

◆ Offending your supervisor.

To avoid these causes of failure you must:

◆ Prepare thoroughly for the session.

◆ Listen carefully to what your supervisor has to say.

◆ Answer objections adequately (in detail, but just enough to hold your supervisor's attention and interest).

◆ If possible, turn objections around so that they become reasons to accept your arguments. For example, if your supervisor points out that you have been on the job only six months, you might respond that, far from seeing your work as routine, you still retain your original enthusiasm and high motivation.

◆ Avoid cockiness, sarcasm, and overt hostility.

◆ Dress neatly and appropriately.

◆ Maintain a positive attitude toward what is being said: listen attentively, and be alert and responsive.

◆ Present strong and convincing arguments.

◆ Display interest and enthusiasm.

◆ Be strong but *not* overpowering.

Chapter 8

You as a Negotiator

"You win by trying, not by standing around!"
—Fran Tarkenton

Now it's time to take a look at you, especially in the role of negotiator. What kind of appearance do you present to your supervisor? What kind of signals do you project by your body language? Are you alert to the signals being conveyed to you? To complete this personal appraisal, consider your behavior during the negotiation session, including self-evaluation of how you did.

PRINCIPLE 8

> *Stop: look at and listen to yourself, and visualize how others see you.*

1. Your Appearance Counts

When you look into a mirror, you get a certain impression about yourself. To obtain the raise you deserve, you want that image to reflect a positive-type person, one who is alert but not tense and one who can meet challenges. You've got to look confident that you can convince your supervisor you're more than worth every dollar the company pays you.

For this reason, your physical appearance as a negotiator is of utmost importance. How you dress will reflect your personality, credibility, and appropriate management position. A dark suit or dress conveys authority, but black should be avoided—it's too negative. Long-sleeved shirts or blouses are more appropriate than short-sleeved ones. Shoes should be styled conservatively (no sneakers!), free from scuffs, and color-coordinated with the rest of the outfit. Here's a common sense rule: To negotiate a raise, dress slightly more, not less, conservatively than your supervisor.

Eye contact connotes friendship, trust, and self-confidence, but staring may indicate hostility and disrespect. A warm smile is fine, but it should be sincere, not a mechanical display of teeth. Since dry lips show fear and tension, keep your lips moist. Coughing often projects nervousness unless, of course, you obviously have a cold. Have a clean handkerchief handy to cover unexpected sneezes.

Special Advice for Men
Your dress code should follow the next level in your organization. Regardless of how you dress, make sure your clothes are neat and

clean. If suits are the norm, start with a solid navy or dark gray suit. You may vary your look by the shirt styles or neckwear you choose. Solid suits are more appropriate than pinstripes. Wear a long sleeve shirt with your suit. Dress shirts themselves should be cotton and polyester blends. A 100 percent cotton shirt may feel better but may look like a mess of wrinkles by the time you arrive at work.

Stick with white shirts. A conservative tie is proper. Socks should be dark and should not sag around the ankles. Shoes should always look shined and heels should not be worn out. Jewelry should be kept to a minimum.

Special Advice for Women

Women have an easier time than men in putting a wardrobe together, since their range of acceptable business attire is broader. Women are not always forced to wear business suits, but they must dress conservatively. Shades of gray or blue, or earth tones are appropriate; avoid reds, bright yellow, and so on. As advised for men, look at the next level up for guidance.

Women may be criticized for wearing heavy perfume, too much makeup, or too much jewelry. Therefore, women should be conservative in these three areas.

2. Speech Is Important Too

A well-modulated tone—but not monotone—and crisp pronunciation of words, without slurring, will help in projecting a good impression. Clear diction and a proper command of language, including use of an adequate vocabulary and proper grammar, are essential. However, don't attempt to impress your supervisor by using six-syllable words when simple language will put your message across. And remember: never raise your voice, especially if you are angry.

3. Watching for Body Language

Body language may be used to project a person's true personality or to convey false signals. The primary component of body language is eye contact. Prolonged scrutiny can make you feel ill at ease. In contrast, if a listener continually glances in other directions while you are talking, he or she is either disturbed by what you are saying or is not paying full attention. Continual blinking can indicate anger, excitement, or fear. Eyebrow twitching reflects nervousness.

Facial gestures and head movements can also project feelings or thoughts. Cocking the head may indicate interest or doubt. A warm smile usually denotes friendliness and agreement; a frown, sadness or anger.

Using eyeglasses as a prop, such as putting them in one's mouth, usually occurs when a decision is required. You should avoid peering over your glasses, as this can make the other person nervous.

Other types of body language include hand signals (clenched or opened fists) and arm and leg movements. A firm handshake indicates confidence; the "bone-crusher" may show insecurity; and the wet and clammy handshake reflects nervousness. Clenched fists often show anger and hostility. A tapping foot betrays impatience. Arm gestures, such as folding them across the chest, may send a strong signal that threatens the other person. One arm folded in front of your chest with the hand clutching the other arm attempts to disguise nervousness. Leg positions can also project signals. Crossed legs indicate tension, whereas stretched legs (for men) and legs with knees together (for women) show a relaxed attitude.

Many of us, as well prepared as we are, walk into a meeting with sweaty palms and shaky limbs. What can be done? We can try relaxing through deep breathing, or projecting confidence by believing in ourselves. But even the most experienced negotiator feels stress when worrying about the outcome. Some stress-raisers can also play havoc on one's nerves, such as: (1) where you may be seated (perhaps the sun is streaming through a window, right into your eyes); (2) you may be seated in a chair where one leg is shorter than the others; (3) you may discover that you have several people in your audience, rather than a one-on-one situation; and (4) the cup of coffee offered to you may be put into your shaking hand.

How do we cope with such circumstances? If the sun is annoying you, look for a spot in the shade. Relocate your chair and move without mumbling any apology to your supervisor. If your chair is wobbly, tell the supervisor that you'd like to change chairs to a more stable one. Meeting with more than one person can be intimidating. Reply to questions by looking the individual asking the question right in the eyes. Finally, it's best to refuse coffee—but if you do accept a cup, put it down on a sturdy base.

In *Winning by Negotiation,* Dr. Tessa Warschaw emphasizes that you must "pay attention to how you move" and watch your "signals and styles." "Signals are like magnets," she says, "putting out positive and negative energy that either attracts or repels other people." Intimidation signals force others to listen, or control when these others may speak: ". . . raise your eyebrows or throw hard glances to express disapproval, turn your body away if you don't like what is being said, rise, read a memo on your desk or start to make a phone call when you want to end the meeting." A desire for solitude is shown by silence: "involuntary signals include facial and body twitches, jiggling legs and knees, nervous hands." Signs of approval include nodding one's head, flashing friendly glances, and the like. "But if your intent is to create a dialogue," Dr. Warschaw emphasizes, "your expressions will convey concern and care and genuine interest, and you'll give the other person the time needed to respond."

As you will have surmised by now, body language is a course in itself; it involves studying details of movement that are much more intricate than those described here. Much of what we know about this fascinating subject is learned by experience.

4. "How Did I Do?"

Self-assessment will help you to gain insight into your personality traits and your skills as a negotiator. By employing a checklist, it is possible to determine how well the negotiation was conducted and, in particular, how you appeared to your supervisor.

During the session, did you:

◆ follow your plan as you had prepared it?

◆ let your supervisor finish speaking without interrupting?

◆ avoid being offensive or argumentative? (This is where the "Yes, but . . ." technique may have come in handy.)

◆ answer questions directly without deviating from your salary objectives?

◆ avoid making concessions out of fear?

◆ pay careful attention to your body language:

◆ avoid distracting mannerisms such as tapping your fingers or a pencil, wringing your hands, fidgeting, and touching your face?

  – avoid obvious reactions to tension such as yawning, twitching, and perspiring?

  – speak firmly and lucidly in a crisp, friendly, and audible tone?

  – control the manner of presentation so that you appeared cordial and self-confident but not arrogant?

  – observe the signals that indicated:

  – how friendly your supervisor felt upon greeting you?

  – when you should stop your presentation?

Chapter 9

Case Studies:

Do's and Don'ts in Negotiating a Raise

"However toplofty and idealistic a man may be, he can always rationalize his right to earn money."

—Raymond Chandler
in a letter to his literary agent

Let's consider three common situations that may be encountered in salary administration: getting an acceptable salary increase, getting a raise before it's due, and negotiating a raise that accompanies a promotion.

PRINCIPLE 9

There's a right way and a wrong way. Once you find the right way, stick with it!

In all of the cases illustrated below, the two parties are identified as follows:

E = Employee
S = Supervisor

Before delving into the three case studies, let's review what we've learned so far about negotiating salaries.

◆ "I went into my supervisor's office, anticipating a satisfactory raise, but I was told I was getting a minimal one."

◆ They'll do better next year.

◆ "It was frustrating and I thought there was nothing I could do to change his mind."

Managers often tell employees that they have a limited amount of money to spread around the department. However, managers do divert money to those they think are underpaid or to reward top performers. If you are disappointed with your raise, tell your supervisor you'd like to be considered for a larger rather than a minimal raise before the next review period. Remind your supervisor about the excellent work you've done, how it will save the company money, and why you believe you are entitled to a larger raise. Point out how quickly you've learned the work, how well you fit into the corporate structure, and how you'd like to be able to accomplish more. Identify those projects that, with your contributions, could be of added value to the company. Always remember to remain professional during a salary review.

Before you leap into a job with another company, review what your current company's future may represent and how you'd fit in. Then consider the same factors for the future of the prospective company.

Is there a promotion in sight where you are now that would provide a substantial rather than a moderate raise to help compensate
for your patience?

A difficult part of the salary negotiation meeting is stating what
you want and why you deserve it. Thus, preparation is the key to
overcoming the obstacles to success. Make notes after researching
salary trends and other statistical material. Bring your activity log
book to the meeting to back up discussions about your worth to
the company. Demonstrate an air of success in your dress and man-
nerism. Avoid taking notes during the meeting, but afterwards, log
the sequence of events and results in your journal.

Look to the future

Discuss your expectations for the next year, including benefits and
perks. Ask questions about risks in the future of the project you're
involved in, such as: Where will I be in five years? What are the
future plans of the company and how will I be included? How long
has my supervisor been with this company, on the project, in his or
her current position?

Overcoming salary objections

The three most common objections of your supervisor in the area
of salary are as follows:

1. "There's a limited amount of money in the budget for a raise at
   this time."

   Assuming you are in the midpoint of your range, there may be
   another 20 percent available before you reach the top of your
   range. However, your supervisor may be easily convinced that
   you are worthy of an above-average raise, provided you can

demonstrate to him or her that you have better-than-average skills and are valuable to the company. But if you're at the top of the range, shoot for a promotion. However, be careful. Do not give the impression that you want your supervisor's job, unless it can push him or her into the next higher level of supervision. Supervisors should have the latitude to provide higher salaries to retain top-notch skilled individuals.

2. "Some of your peers with education and experience similar to yours don't make as much as you do."

Your emphasis should be that you are an individual who brings more value to the company than the average individual in a similar position.

3. "In your previous position, you weren't earning anywhere close to the salary we'll be paying you in your new position."

You should expect to be compensated for the quality of your performance. If you were paid lower in a previous position, maybe you were not as valuable to the company as you are now. You should emphasize how you have helped the company reach certain objectives, such as increased revenues and profit. Hence, the higher end of the range for your new position should be considered.

CASE 1. GETTING AN ACCEPTABLE SALARY
               INCREASE

The Wrong Way

E: Say, Mr. S, can we get together? I'd like to discuss getting a raise.

S: Sure, why not? Come into my office now.

E: I haven't had a raise for a year. How about it? Aren't I past due?

S: It just so happens your raise is in the works, and you'll get it next month.

E: That's great! Now I have something to look forward to!

(*Critique:* So what went wrong? She got a raise! *But* she didn't bother finding out how much it was, nor was she prepared to negotiate to increase the amount if it was inadequate.)

The Negotiated Way
(The Preliminary)

E: Mr. S, at your convenience, I would like to discuss with you something of importance to both of us.

S: What is it?

E: I'd rather not discuss it out in the open because it's a private matter. If you could set up a time that is convenient to you, I'd appreciate it. It shouldn't take more than 15 minutes.

S: How about 3 o'clock this afternoon in my office?

E: Thank you, that would be fine.

(The meeting)

E: Mr. S, I haven't had an increase in salary in quite a while. Up to now, I was getting raises on an annual basis, but it has been more than a year since my last one. What's going on?

S: As you are aware, E, the company's profits have been down and the immediate future doesn't look too bright. As a result, the interval between raises has been extended.

E: As you know, I've been a loyal employee. But if the company is in such a predicament, perhaps it's risky to remain here. Don't misunderstand me, I want to stay with the company for many years to come, but I expect some recognition and remuneration in return.

S: You know I've been satisfied with you. In fact, I put you in for a raise, but it has been delayed along with the others. Let me see if I can get salary administration to expedite its approval. I'll get back to you as soon as I can.

E: Before we break off this meeting, can you give me an indication of how much of a raise I can expect and when it will be in my paycheck?

S: Sure, the increase is for X, and it will be included in your paycheck one month from the time of approval.

E: But, Mr. S, that increase is less than the cost-of-living increase for the year. I feel I deserve more based on my record.

S: What amount did you have in mind?

E: (*E is prepared with an acceptable salary range and now cites the top figure. He also provides backup by referring to his activity log book, which shows outstanding job performance and other positive factors.*)

S: I must admit that I wasn't aware of all the outstanding things you've done over the past year, and I certainly don't want to lose you. I'll tell you what I'll do: I'll try to bump your raise up to $Y. Is that satisfactory?

E: That's better, but it still falls $Z short of what I'd consider satisfactory. *(Even though $Y falls within the bottom of the acceptable salary range, E tries a higher counteroffer.)*

S: In that case, I think perhaps we may have to delay your raise until the next scheduled review. If you wait another few months, we may be able to get you a little more than $Y, but I can't guarantee it!

E: *(Thinking to himself: I had better quit while I'm ahead. A bird in the hand is worth two in the bush. Get that raise now, and plan for a better one in the future.)* Although I believe—and it looks as though you recognize—that I deserve a larger raise, in consideration of the company's dilemma I'll accept the $Y raise for now. Thank you in advance for any future efforts to provide more adequate increases! I certainly will be in there pitching to get the company over the hurdle. Please let me know when I can help and how.

S: Thank you for your consideration and cooperation. Keep up the good work, and together with the top-notch efforts of the other managers, we will help the company get over this tough time.

(*Critique:* In this example, the first offer is shown not to be the final one. Some employees believe a supervisor's offer is locked into one number, regardless of a company's financial position. Often, it is intimidating for an employee to make a counteroffer, especially if he or she likes the job and plans to stay for a long time. Nevertheless, there is always an opportunity to negotiate, particularly if done cooperatively without creating friction.)

CASE 2. GETTING A RAISE BEFORE IT'S DUE

The Wrong Way

E: Ms. S, this inflation is killing me: fuel prices keep rising, the cost of electricity is up, and the damn taxes just rose another 10 percent. I need a raise just to meet these increases.

S: I would like to give you a raise, but my departmental budget won't permit it. You've been here long enough to know that raises are given only on an annual basis.

E: I figured that would be your answer, but I decided to take a chance and ask you anyway!

(*Critique:* E was unprepared for the meeting (he should have been ready to argue his worth to the company) and gave up too soon.)

The Negotiated Way

E: In the six months since my last salary review, I have taken over the responsibilities of Mr. X as well as retaining my own duties. Since he left the department, you turned over his accounts to me. While this additional work is challenging and I enjoy it, I believe it warrants additional compensation.

S: I certainly appreciate your taking on a bigger workload and the satisfactory performance you continue to demonstrate. But there is no money available for raises at this time.

E: Nevertheless, as we are both aware, Ms. S, the company's revenues and profits are up sharply from last year. I feel that my work contributed to these increases and that a raise is justifiable for me at this time.

S: You've been here long enough to know that the company's policy is to award raises only once a year, and we're only halfway through that period.

E: But we both know that policies can be bent. Suppose someone decides to leave? Wouldn't management provide an interim raise to keep a good worker? Don't get me wrong. I don't want to leave. I like it here and enjoy my work.

S: Well, we could make an exception for a special case, but yours is not unusual.

E: Isn't it a special case if an employee is not being paid in accordance with what he is contributing? My workload has increased immensely, and I've taken on the additional responsibilities without griping. I know I'm doing an excellent job, and I'm sure the company and especially you want to continue to treat me fairly.

S: Others in our department are contributing more than what is expected of their positions, and they're satisfied; they aren't asking for raises.

E: *(At this point, the activity log is displayed and thumbed through.)* I'm sure that you can be proud of your department's output, but I cannot speak for others. The extra work I've undertaken imposes more responsibilities for additional skills and requires devoting spare time to study things more carefully.

S: I guess I haven't fully realized the situation and its impact on your workload. Give me some time to talk it over with salary administration to see whether there's a chance of getting an interim raise for you. I'll get back to you within the week.

E: Thank you, Ms. S, I appreciate your consideration.

(The next meeting, a week later)

S: I'm pleased to inform you that you are being considered for a promotion and, of course, an accompanying raise within the normal review period. But in appreciation of your excellent performance, I have stressed to salary administration that you have earned a raise and they concurred to grant an interim increase of $X. I hope this is satisfactory.

E: I really am pleased, *especially* in looking forward to that promotion! Thank you, Ms. S!

(*Critique:* The supervisor was forced to reveal that a promotion was being considered. Gaining an interim raise on top of a coming promotion certainly was a coup. Also, the employee did not require an extensive effort to convince his boss of the outstanding performance. Probably the activity log helped to promote the interim raise.)

CASE 3. NEGOTIATING THE RAISE ACCOMPANYING A PROMOTION

The Wrong Way

S: I thought that getting the promotion you've been promised would please you. And the increase in salary is indeed commensurate with the new title. I can't understand why you're not satisfied. What salary would you be happy with?

E: I'm making $XX,XXX now and would have expected at least a 10 percent increase.

S: Well, a 6 percent increase is standard policy with any promotion in this company. You do want this promotion, don't you?

E: Sure I do! Oh, well, I guess I'd better be satisfied with the regular increase.

(*Critique:* E gave in too easily and did not show confidence in her own worth.)

The Negotiated Way

S: I thought getting the promotion you've been promised would please you. And the increase in salary is indeed commensurate with the new title. I can't understand why you're not satisfied. What salary would you be happy with?

E: I think you can understand better than anyone else, what raise should accompany a promotion—certainly not one that is just equal to a merit raise. I request that you reconsider what may be suitable.

S: I think you should consider the promotion and not be too concerned with salary. After all, the promotion does place you in another bracket and provides you with a broader salary range and chances for more raises!

E: Certainly you are right, but I don't want to wait another year until the next merit review before getting another raise. I would feel cheated by losing out on a whole year's difference in salary.

S: I hate to think how grumpy you may be until next year when salary review occurs again. Of course, you realize that you wouldn't have gotten this promotion unless I thought you had earned it. So let's hear what salary would satisfy you.

E: Before getting back to the salary, I'd like to know more about my new job responsibilities. Tell me more about how the departmental structure will change and who will report to me. Also, what are some of your plans for the growth of our department in the near and far future?

S: The main objective this coming year is to increase the number of subcontracts and purchase orders we process. For this reason, we are computerizing and automating the issuance of requests for quotations and purchase orders. Some of the people who are your peers in your current position will be reporting to you. You will be performing some of my duties, relieving me of those responsibilities and giving me time to plan the expansion and reorganization of the department.

E: It all sounds great. But let me return to the subject at hand. In the new position, what is the salary range? And, will the frequency of salary reviews be the same as in my current position?

S: Your performance will be appraised and your salary reviewed annually. If you are performing as well as you are doing now, there's no reason not to expect annual increases. As for the range, it has been established by salary administration and falls between $XX,XXX and $XY,YYY. But let me point out that, if you had an MBA, your starting salary for the new position could be on the higher, not the lower, end of the scale.

E: Apparently you're not convinced that I've been doing more than just a satisfactory job. Let's take a moment to review what I've accomplished since the last performance appraisal. (*E's activity log is presented and reviewed; her outstanding accomplishments are emphasized.*) According to my job performance, I think you might agree that the salary should be toward midrange. Certainly my qualifications and accomplishments warrant a better increase than 6 percent.

S: But you don't have an advanced degree, and you must be trained for the new position. The company will provide you with training on company time; that's a major concession.

E: Well, I haven't brought you completely up-to-date on my background. As for the MBA, I expect to complete my studies and be awarded a degree next year. Also, in my spare time, I have been attending various workshops and seminars under the auspices of the NCMA that cover contractual matters.

S: Well, as I said, the company has established $XX,XXX as the starting level for the new position, but let me advise salary administration of your additional qualifications, of which I must admit I was unaware. I'll get back to you later this week.

E: I know that I may have put you in a difficult position, and I do appreciate your efforts. I certainly can wait a week for your response. Thank you.

S: Okay, see you then.

(A phone call two days later)

S: Would it be satisfactory to you if we started you at $XX,XXX with the agreement that you will receive an increase at a level closer to your expectations after a six-month trial period?

E: That sounds fair enough. Thank you.

(*Critique:* This case exemplifies a salary offer-and-counteroffer procedure. Note that E was aware of what constituted a more acceptable percentage for a raise accompanying a promotion. She had done her homework and was prepared to defend her worth. In contrast, S did not prepare adequately and he was unaware of E's pursuit of education. After all, S had been approving company-sponsored tuition-reimbursement checks for E's graduate work for a number of years and should have found out just what E was doing. As E pointed out, the additional training received outside of working hours would be cost-effective in that the company need not conduct a training program for the new job, and E's time could be spent more productively.)

Chapter 10

Analyzing How
You Won That
Raise and Looking
Ahead

"We dare not look back to great yesterdays. We must look forward to great tomorrows."

—Adlai E. Stevenson

After completion of the raise negotiation, which we presume turned out satisfactorily, you should record what transpired by recalling the sequence of events and analyzing what you did right, what you may have done wrong, and what your strong and weak points were as a negotiator. By recording this session in your activity log book, you will immediately prepare yourself for the next salary review and for future sessions. Refer to Chapter 8 and review the question "How Did I Do?"

THE THANK YOU NOTE

An effective negotiator is also a good writer. Immediately after the meeting is over, sit down and write a thank you note to your supervisor, reiterating specific points of agreement and highlighting your assets that are most valuable to the company. Keep the note brief by restricting its length to one page. It's extremely important to be diplomatic in expressing whether you gained or lost ground and politely let your supervisor know that you look forward to future salary reviews. Be positive in tone in looking toward a bright future for yourself and therefore the firm.

PRINCIPLE 10

You got that big raise—now go for a promotion and more raises.

Now ask yourself these additional questions in regard to the negotiation:

◆ Did I review my accomplishments and show how effective I have been in job performance and profitability to the firm?

◆ Did I compare my supervisor's goals against my performance objectives to ensure agreement?

◆ Did I let my supervisor make the first offer for a salary increase and then negotiate a higher figure, using the initial offer as a jumping-off point?

◆ How does the raise compare, over the current year and for the past five years, with:
    (1) cost-of-living adjustment figures,
    (2) production workers' increases,
    (3) unionized workers' increases,
    (4) increases granted to other managerial levels,

    (5) increases for others in the same position, both inside and
        outside the department, and

    (6) increases cited in surveys for my occupation and location?

◆ Were fringe benefits offered, and, if so, what did I accept?

◆ What are the dollar-value equivalents of the fringe benefits I
   accepted?

In Philip Sperber's book *Fail-Safe Business Negotiating,* five strategies for job advancement are identified that may be adapted and
compared with the strategies and tactics you used in negotiating
your raise. It may be helpful to keep Sperber's strategies in mind
(and in your log book) for the next time:

1. You demonstrate that you take on responsibility and are promotable by impressing your supervisor to reach that conclusion.

2. You assist your supervisor by supportive, outstanding (or, at least,
   good) performance to make him or her look good to management.

3. You play to your supervisor's ego and emotional needs so as to
   enhance your chances for a promotion or a better raise.

4. Your performance excels to such a degree that your rating is
   top-notch in the job-appraisal rating system employed by the
   company.

5. You project a good image and make it visible to not only your
   supervisor but also your supervisor's superiors and any other
   member(s) of higher management that you may encounter during the course of performing your job.

In the past, the "organization man" looked forward to a career
that moved upward with promotions coming every two years,
where personal feelings were secondary to corporate support, suc-

cess equated to job security through retirement, "good pay" was age times $1,000, and a 40-hour workweek was standard. Today's manager expects lateral moves as routine (or even desirable), with responsibilities increasing with fewer title changes. Success may equate to salary level more than personal satisfaction, with compensation including bonuses and profit sharing. The manager will probably work until a particular assignment is completed, regardless of the time it may take.

So if your management is following this trend, can you expect more frequent and better raises instead of promotions? That is another consideration and should provide impetus in getting a bigger raise, now and in the future. In the past, salaries and promotions were almost synonymous, and "big" raises accompanied promotions. Today, the emphasis is on compensation in any form—dollars or other comparable benefits.

Management currently expects more from managers in taking on responsibilities in situations where they may receive rewards later (i.e., end-of-the-year bonuses) for demonstrating excellence in performance. But companies may not recognize employee dissatisfaction if there is a lack of employee recognition in the form of promotions, as well as compensation. In times of prosperity, dissatisfaction is manifested by high employee turnover, or an unusual number of middle managers deciding to start their own businesses to satisfy their thirst for accomplishment and recognition. When the economy is recessional, however, companies can demand more from the employees at lower compensation levels. Of course, top management considers profit the number-one priority, even to the point of sacrificing top-notch managers and eliminating strategic-planning departments. This policy may well be shortsighted, since these employees may have been the "brains" of an organization and may have been responsible for reshaping the firm to improve profitability in future years. Today the world is in a hurry—company managers have lost patience and can't wait for higher profits to become visible. A year of lower profits may mean decreased stock prices and a reduction in the value of stock holdings by top management.

So where do you, as a manager, go from here? One sensible course is to improve your negotiation techniques, which not only assist in the attainment of better raises now but also will be valuable in future employment opportunities. As indicated earlier, negotiation techniques are something that everyone can learn to employ as an additional aid for achieving success. Also, the techniques may help to foster a positive mental attitude and provide know-how in responding to negative replies or in converting negative answers into positive ones. For example, if your supervisor said, "You were turned down for a raise because you lack certain experience or qualifications," you might reply, "If I could prove to you that I am qualified, would you give me the increase?" As an effective negotiator, you would be able to keep the dialogue going until a satisfactory response was received.

Chapter 11

You Didn't Get
That Raise,
Now What?

"The highest reward that God gives us for good work is the ability to do better work."

—Elbert Hubbard, author
Selected Writings

In the past, employees rarely worked for more than one company during their careers. In most cases, raises were automatic. Now, with corporations expecting to get the most productivity from each worker, automatic raises are infrequent for managers but are common for unionized workers. Today, managers must think of what action to take when raises are unsatisfactory or chances for promotion are limited. Furthermore, economists believe that corporations in the future will be structured by a core of managers with generalized business backgrounds who will hire temporary workers with specialties as the assignments require.

PRINCIPLE 11

> *Be ready to open the door when opportunity knocks.*

If you are caught in the web of downsizing, what can you do for compensation while seeking new employment or, possibly, a new career? Prior to your exit interview, contemplate achieving some relief by requesting:

◆ assistance in preparing a resume

◆ assistance in searching for a new job

◆ adequate severance pay (this is where your negotiating techniques are really put to the test!)

◆ provision for the interim by the company or via COBRA for long-term permanent health insurance

◆ use of secretarial assistance in preparation of letters to prospective employers

Note that if you are not allowed to leave your 401(k) plan with the company, or you prefer not to, you might roll over the total distribution from that plan into either your new employer's plan or into an IRA. If handled correctly, no additional tax liability will be incurred.

1. Think About Changing Your Career
In addition to downsizing (or layoffs), some other causes for career changes may include:

◆ company-sponsored early retirements via bonuses or "golden parachutes"

◆ burnout

◆ forced retirement

◆ a promotion awarded to someone else

◆ voluntary (i.e., having no further opportunities available; having reached a level of competency: or having a prospective business opportunity)

Robert Otterbourg's book *It's Never Too Late: 150 Men and Women Who Changed Their Careers* contains a survey of individuals with encouraging stories. "Career changers are alike in other ways. Most show a willingness to set aside rank and title to start their new careers...More than any other factors, the twin effects of corporate downsizing and early retirement are helping to enlarge the pool of career changes. Some career changers dipped into savings, were supported by spouses, reduced their material needs, or used the proceeds from the sale of a business…"

Examples of reported career changers extracted from this book include:

◆ A medical engineer who sold a high-tech electronics company and went into a mail-order business.

◆ A research chemist who opened a bed and breakfast inn.

◆ A company executive with an MBA degree who became a director of a nonprofit community action group.

◆ An investment banker who became a professor of international banking at a college.

◆ A microbiologist for a pharmaceutical company who became a science teacher.

◆ A chemical engineer for a large company who became an associate dean in a university's school of engineering, handling administrative matters.

◆ An assistant vice president for an insurance company who became a teacher of mathematics and science in a university.

◆ An advertising agency executive who became a lawyer.

◆ A software engineer who became a journalist.

◆ A nuclear physicist who became a cartoonist.

If you are contemplating a career change, think about the following items:

◆ Use your business or vocational experience.

◆ Review and weigh the direction your career is heading.

◆ Test your aptitude.

◆ Network with professionals and attend workshops.

◆ Explore the market for current and future needs.

◆ Further your education.

◆ Gather facts, weighing the costs against potential positions and salaries today and in the future.

How you succeed in this dynamic and ever-changing economy is up to you. You first must consider that any career is linked to education and skill levels. Most likely, any earning power depends upon what you have learned on the job as well. Having connections both within and outside your field is always helpful. Keeping up-to-date with technology, new products and services, needs within your company or industry, and with the economy in general should become second nature to you. Think of your career, your company, your industry, and the economy as integrated parts of the entire workplace. In many cases, teamwork may boost, rather than hinder, the quality of your individual performance.

Management skills can be developed through experience. Sharing information about opportunities, making contact with your peers via networking, and keeping continual contact with fellow professionals within your industry should become your working lifestyle.

THINK BEFORE YOU LEAP

In changing careers, it's very tempting to start your own business. But before charging into this endeavor, think of the chances of succeeding. Government statistics show that on an annual basis, almost a million businesses are started. Many of them fail, but if a business survives its first five years, its chances of success are high. Before starting a business, review your prospect for success: Do you have enough capital to carry you through the business's infancy? Do you have a product or service that will fill the needs of the users? Do you have an adequate business plan, ranging from the beginning over a five-year duration? Do you have the means to distribute your product? The three biggest culprits in causing business failure are undercapitalization, inadequate marketing capability, and one's inexperience or lack of knowledge about a product or industry.

In researching employment opportunities, keep in mind the desirability of finding:

◆ A company that offers a profit-sharing plan.

◆ A company that allows the freedom to express opinions, especially in improving business by minimizing costs and increasing profitability.

◆ A company that offers retirement plans.

◆ A company that provides health care insurance as a basic benefit to an individual and to one's family.

◆ A business that is family oriented and offers programs for the well-being of the individuals, which may also result in the well-being of the organization.

◆ A company that is committed to assisting its employees in furthering their education or knowledge and skills.

◆ A company that may offer retraining programs to personnel who are slated for layoff.

Kathryn and Ross Petras' book *Jobs '96* provides information regarding jobs, industries, and regional trends as related to careers. Furthermore, it lists salaries and prospective firms, and is divided into three sections: career, industry, and regional. For example, an excerpt from the book is provided below for a career as a manager:

"How to succeed in the second half of the '90s:

◆ be multilingual

◆ be a generalist with technical skills

◆ be computer literate

◆ be a doer, not a follower

◆ be a team player, or be a leader."

Recognize the following germane items:

- Competition is tougher now than it ever was.

- Corporations are global.

- Corporations are more involved with government and public projects.

- Corporations are looking for:
  - broader responsibility of individuals
  - greater number of people reporting to one person
  - computer competency

- Education: An MBA from a top-notch school may help you to advance.

- These are growing fields of opportunity: management consulting, health care, supermarket chains, hotel management, computers, financial management, property and facilities management.

Before changing your career, research opportunities elsewhere. Subscribe to a trade or professional magazine in the field of interest, join a professional society and attend seminars, keep your resume up-to-date and read books on business and career-related subjects.

If you decide to remain in your current position, you must learn to love your job. Make working a learning process: learn how to cooperate and how to communicate, expand your area of expertise and responsibility, learn from mistakes, and balance your life to enjoy the time at and away from work.

2. Industries/Occupations with Bright Futures

Technology, especially with the advent of the computer age, has widened the salary gap between well-educated, technical workers and those lacking education and skills to compete. Average wages for newer technical jobs are higher than for existing jobs. Those workers with older technological skills are the ones caught in downsizing or perhaps being forced to accept cuts in salary. Thus, workers must continually retrain or reeducate themselves to become more viable in a job market whose needs are constantly changed by improved technology.

Taking into account current trends in employment opportunities, consider the following career prospects:

◆ Health care—Demand for workers in hospitals is decreasing, but with the emphasis on managed health care, in-home care and out-patient clinics will grow. Investigate careers in therapy, pathology, medical record management, and veterinary medicine.

◆ Law—Demand for attorneys will increase but competition will make employment as a lawyer tough. However, there may be more opportunities for legal support services (e.g., paralegals).

◆ Engineering—This field can still be considered cyclical with its ups and downs decade by decade. However, environmental engineering may be considered the top engineering specialty.

◆ Accounting—Its outlook is considered good.

◆ Education—Because of two-income families, child care positions are on the rise. In the near future, opportunities in this field include special education teachers, language teachers, and high school teachers.

◆ Communications—This field is still in its infancy. The information superhighway and multimedia technology provide opportunities.

◆ Marketing—Growth potentials in marketing include advertising and public relations.

◆ Science—Labor shortages exist for physical and medical scientists, computer specialists, and geologists Look to math-oriented positions such as actuary, statistician, biologist, physicist, and astronomer.

LOOK FOR JOB OPENINGS WITHIN YOUR FIRM

Job positions provide you with information on opportunities that are available in your company. Exploring these opportunities can help you determine what you may want to go after and prepare yourself with the skills and background material needed prior to an interview. Make sure it is what you want and that you fit in.

If your firm has performance reviews, and you are knowledgeable about any job posted, you may take advantage during the review to bring it to your boss' attention. Also, a mutual discussion may be in order to review your career objectives and how they relate to the job posted. (More about performance reviews was covered in Chapter 5.)

WHAT ABOUT DOWNSIZED WORKERS RETURNING AS TEMPORARY HELP?

There are four categories of workers (as defined by the Bureau of Labor Statistics) who have returned to their permanent employer under non-permanent employment arrangements. The are:

◆ on-call workers

◆ temporary help agency workers

◆ workers provided by contract firms

◆ independent contractors, paid wages or salaries

The use of these types of workers is quite common, and many companies have found their use cost-effective. On one hand, they don't want to lose experienced personnel, but, on the other hand, they don't want to pay them as careerists. So they've initiated this "revolving door" policy by using experienced workers as needed. Some former employees have increased wages, whereas others receive lower wages than when they were full-time employees. Company benefits are a thing of the past for them.

3. Anticipated Salaries

Salaries may be correlated to industrial growth. In comparing a few major industries, information gleaned from the Bureau of Labor Statistics shows the average annual industrial growth rate as follows:

The "Winners":

◆ Business Services	+6.7%
◆ Brokerage	+5.6
◆ Transportation Services	+4.4
◆ Furniture Stores	+3.4
◆ Health Services	+3.3
◆ Engineering & Management	+3.1
◆ Education	+3.0
◆ State & Local Government	+1.5

The "Losers":

◆ Printing & Publishing	−0.3
◆ Chemicals	−0.9
◆ Apparel & Accessory Stores	−1.1

◆ Utility Services   −1.2

◆ Federal Government   −1.2

◆ Banks & Savings Institutions   −1.7

◆ Apparel & Textile   −2.8

◆ Leather   −4.8

On a more regional basis, let's review statistics from the Florida Department of Labor and Employment Security, Division of Jobs and Benefits (Bureau of Labor Market Statistics), which has provided wage data for selected occupations in Dade, Broward, and Palm Beach Counties. This state survey helps both employees and employers with salary information—what one can expect as the average wage, minimum and maximum wages. A limited list follows:

Occupation	Hourly Wages		
	Average	Minimum	Maximum
Accountants	$18.88	$8.50	$50.00
Building Inspectors	16.84	7.51	25.39
Chemical Engineers	35.66	14.42	45.00
Civil Engineers	23.81	12.62	45.66
Computer Engineers	21.02	10.00	35.58
Computer Programmers	18.82	9.28	30.77
Electrical/Electronic Engineers	19.66	10.00	40.41
Financial Managers	26.62	10.00	62.00
Industrial Engineers	19.91	9.87	34.25
Industrial Production Managers	20.95	10.00	40.34
Management Analysts	22.01	8.00	38.46
Mechanical Engineers	20.28	10.00	38.47
Municipal Clerks	17.49	10.47	26.58
Occupational Therapists	23.41	11.02	35.00

Occupation	Hourly Wages		
	Average	Minimum	Maximum
Office Managers	15.66	5.00	32.69
Personnel Relations Managers	17.35	8.50	39.66
Physical Therapists	22.95	10.07	36.00
Purchasing Managers	19.68	9.43	36.06
Software Engineers	20.18	10.00	38.46
Systems Analysts, EDP	18.96	9.00	35.30

These statistics, which are issued annually, can provide data to assist you in knowing limitations in each occupation. The federal government and each state provides comparable statistics that you can draw upon to know where you stand. Naturally, the statistic that is most difficult to provide is missing: salary vs. years of experience.

4. Networking to Develop Contacts for Employment

In Cynthia Chin-Lee's book *It's Who You Know: Career Strategies for Making Effective Personal Contacts*, she advises how to maximize networking efforts by:

♦ **Teaching.** Increase your visibility by teaching part or full time in or relative to your field of expertise.

♦ **Public Speaking.** Volunteer to give seminars or speeches in your field, in particular, at your professional society or career fairs.

♦ **Consulting.** Full or part time, provides many contacts.

♦ **Publishing articles or books.** Contribute articles to the company newsletter, local papers, and regional and trade publications. Publishing a book—if you can—leads to more overall exposure.

◆ **Becoming a Leader of a Volunteer Organization.** Gives you a chance to practice management skills as well as increase your visibility in the organization and community.

◆ **Running for Public Office.** Whether in a professional organization or political, athletic, or community organization, this provides additional exposure.

By networking, you can enhance your self-image, your appearance, your mannerisms, and your speech. All of these lead to positive attitudes that can only assist you. Your improvement will reflect on your desirability in either your current or future position. Meeting people, helping them, and letting them help you is most enriching.

5. Seeking New Employment

As an experienced manager, you are not a neophyte in knowing how to seek employment. However, it may have been some time since you have job-hunted and your skills may be rusty. Thus, it's beneficial to review techniques in preparing resumes, passing tests required by employers, and conducting successful interviews.

When applying for a job, you must provide sufficient information for the prospective employer to evaluate your skills and qualifications. A resume is in order when applying for management level, professional, or technical positions. Your resume should include: the type of position you seek, your educational background and professional experience. In describing your professional experience, you should include positions you held, your duties and responsibilities, identification of companies, and dates of employment. Also, include special skills (such as honors received, awards from professional societies, knowledge of special techniques, and proficiency in foreign languages.) The resume should be accompanied by a cover letter addressed to the person being contacted (with his or her title). In the letter, explain the reason for your interest in the company, a brief summary of your qualifications (especially, why you'd be an asset to the company), and a request for an interview.

For some positions, tests may be required such as aptitude tests, job knowledge and proficiency tests, literacy tests, physical ability tests, medical examinations, drug tests, and personality tests, to name a few. Before taking any particular test, learn about the testing process employed by the prospective employer. Brush up on job skills. For example: practice typing in preparation for a typing (proficiency) test; review books covering specific skills; do exercises in preparation for physical ability tests; review reading and mathematics books in preparation for literacy tests. Some help may be found in books covering preparation for civil service jobs. (Check your local library.)

Prior to any job interview, learn as much as you can about the company (from annual reports, product descriptions, etc.) the position's salary and benefits, the prospective job requirements, and how well you qualify for the position. Dress according to the guidelines described in Chapter 8.

During the interview, express your interest in the company. Most importantly, let the interviewer direct the conversation. Answer all questions clearly. Show how your background will make you productive in a short time. Speak positively of your former employers. Negotiate your salary (see previous discussions on this subject) at subsequent meetings.

If you do not receive an offer on the spot, ask when a decision will be made. (You may be requested to return for a second interview— a positive sign.) After thanking your interviewer, reaffirm your interest by reemphasizing your qualifications.

Make an analysis of how well your interview went. Each interview should be treated as a learning experience. Thus, review and list specific ways for improvement. Don't get discouraged!

Career Information on the Internet

Some companies, professional societies, academic institutions, and government agencies maintain online resources (via the Internet) that are updated regularly on organizational activities. Information may include government documents, schedules of events, job openings, and networking contacts. Academic institutions provide links to career counseling and placement services.

As may be done in a library search, various lists may be examined by field or discipline or by using particular keywords. A book titled *The Internet Yellow Pages* is available in many libraries and may assist you in finding an Internet subject.

6. Contemplating Relocation when Changing Jobs

When considering a career change, whether it be to work for a new company or take a new job in your current company you should evaluate how relocation may affect the salary level. In particular, you should investigate regions where potential job growth is positive and avoid regions where there is little growth or a downturn in hiring. To lure talent to fill slots for which it is tough to find qualified workers, out-of-town companies will place want ads in local newspapers, or register with employment agencies and executive search firms. These companies may also use the Internet to recruit high-level specialists. Also, temporary-employment agencies may be used to fill low-end jobs. They may count on word-of-mouth, offering incentives to their employees who help recruit qualified workers.

In reviewing the job market we must consider statistics that reveal geographic changes during this decade. It should come as no surprise that it shows job growth has been distributed unevenly across the country. Many jobs have been created in the metropolitan areas of the Sun Belt, whereas the Northeast is predominantly a downsized market.

The Bureau of Labor Statistics provides the ranking of metropolitan areas by the number of jobs gained or lost and the growth rate over the period from 1991 to 1996. A list is provided for information and is limited to the top ten areas. For other areas being considered for relocation, you may obtain additional information from the Bureau.

Top 10 Metropolitan Areas by Job Gain

	Five-year Job Gain	Annual Growth Rate
Atlanta	371,300	4.5%
Chicago	296,400	1.6
Phoenix	243,100	4.4
Dallas	223,000	3.0
Detroit	197,500	2.0
Minneapolis-St. Paul	178,400	2.5
Boston	174,000	1.3
Houston	162,300	1.9
Denver	160,500	3.5
Las Vegas	157,500	6.6

Top 10 Metropolitan Areas by Growth Rate

	Five-year Job Gain	Annual Growth Rate
Las Vegas, NV	157,500	6.6%
Austin, TX	139,300	6.2
Boise, ID	46,900	6.0
Fayetteville, AK	31,600	5.6
Provo, UT	28,900	5.3
Killeen-Temple, TX	21,800	5.3
Salt Lake City, UT	134,000	4.8
Albuquerque, NM	68,900	4.7
Boulder, CO	30,200	4.6
Atlanta, GA	371,300	4.5

Top 10 Metropolitan Areas by Job Loss

Los Angeles	−194,400	−1.0%
New York	−108,100	−0.6
Hartford	−24,600	−0.8
San Francisco	−22,000	−0.5
Honolulu	−9,700	−0.5
Philadelphia	−8,300	−0.5
Binghamton, NY	−5,900	−1.0
Santa Barbara, CA	−4,900	−0.7
Bakersfield, CA	−3,800	−0.4
Bergen-Passaic, NJ	−3,300	−0.1

Another major factor to consider when contemplating relocation is cost of living. An analysis may be made for annual costs by comparing your current location to the region under consideration. Compare taxes (school, local, and state), housing costs (rental or purchase prices), food, clothing, transportation, insurance, utilities, entertainment, and club memberships.

In examining executive-level salary statistics for primary metropolitan areas, salaries may be compared on a percentage basis. By using a salary level of 100 percent for the average town or city, the influence of the cost of living for the following cited areas is evident:

San Francisco	145.7%
Los Angeles	131.7
New York	126.7
Washington, DC	121.7
Boston	118.3
Philadelphia	111.7
Detroit	109.0
Chicago	107.7
Houston	96.0
Dallas	95.7

In other words, executives in San Francisco should earn, on average, 45.7 percent more than those in most other cities, to compensate for the high cost of living there. Here again, further information is available from the Bureau of Labor Statistics for more metropolitan areas for you to examine.

THE AUTHOR'S PRINCIPLES FOR NEGOTIATING RAISES

1. *If a CEO is worth millions, certainly a company can well afford to reward a middle manager adequate raises.*

2. *Know your adversary.*

3. *Job relevancy is important, but personal achievement is better.*

4. *Job evaluations and appraisals may measure managerial performance, but without adequate raises they are meaningless.*

5. *Plan your moves; then move your plans.*

6. *You probably won't get everything you ask for, but you can surely try!*

7. *To be considered successful, a salary negotiation should leave both parties feeling as though they have won something; you, a satisfactory raise; your supervisor, a contented, productive manager.*

8. *Stop: look at and listen to yourself, and visualize how others see you.*

9. *There's a right way and a wrong way. Once you find the right way, stick with it!*

10. *You got that big raise—now go for a promotion and more raises.*

11. *Be ready to open the door when opportunity knocks.*

SUGGESTED READING

Aldrich, Mark and Robert Buchele, *The Economics of Comparable Worth*. Cambridge, MA: Ballinger Publishing Co., 1986.

Anderson, Kare, *Getting What You Want, How to Reach Agreement and Resolve Conflict Every Time*. New York: Dutton, 1993.

Baber, Anne and Waymon, *How to Fireproof Your Career, Survival Strategies for Volatile Times*. New York: Berkley Books, 1995.

Barkley, Nella and Eric Sandburg, *The Crystal-Barkley Guide to Taking Charge of Your Career*. New York: Workman Publishing, 1995.

Beier, Ernst G. and Evans G. Valens, *People-Reading*. New York: Warner Books, 1989.

Berne, Eric, *Games People Play*. New York: Grove Press, 1985.

Chapman, Jack, *How to Make $1,000 a Minute: Negotiating Salaries and Raises*. Berkeley, CA: Ten Speed Press, 1987.

Chastain, Sherry, *Winning the Salary Game*. New York: John Wiley & Sons, 1980.

Chin-Lee, Cynthia, *It's Who You Know: Career Strategies for Making Effective Personal Contacts*. San Marco, CA: Avant Books, 1991.

Fritz, Dr. Roger, *How to Manage Your Boss*. Hawthorne, NJ: Career Press, 1994.

Hartman, George M., *Making the Deal, Quick Tips for Successful Negotiating*. New York: John Wiley & Sons, 1992.

Karrass, Chester L., *Give and Take*. New York: Thomas Y. Crowell, 1993.

_____, *The Negotiating Game*. New York: Thomas Y. Crowell, 1994.

Kennedy, Joyce Lance, *Higher Salaries: How to Get Them*. Cardiff, CA: Sun Features, 1983.

McCormack, Mark H., *What They Still Don't Teach You at Harvard Business School*. New York: Bantam Books, 1989.

Murnighan, J. Keith, *Bargaining Games—A New Approach to Strategic Thinking in Negotiation*. New York: William Morrow & Co., 1992.

Otterbourg, Robert K., *It's Never Too Late: 150 Men and Women Who Changed Their Careers*. New York: Barron's, 1993.

Pease, Allan, *Signals: How to Use Body Language for Power, Success and Love*. New York: Bantam Books, 1984.

Petras, Kathryn and Ross, *Jobs '96*. New York: Simon and Schuster, 1995.

Sartwell, Matthew, Editor, *Napoleon Hill's Key to Success: The 17 Principles of Personal Achievement*. New York: Dutton, 1994.

Schatzki, M. and W. R. Coffey, *Negotiation: The Art of Getting What You Want*. New York: Signet Books, 1981.

Sperber, Philip, *Fail-Safe Business Negotiating*. Englewood Cliffs, NJ: Prentice-Hall, 1983.

Tarkenton, Fran, *Playing to Win*. New York: Harper & Row, 1984.

Warschaw, Tessa A., *Winning by Negotiation*. New York: McGraw-Hill, 1980.

APPENDIX

Software Programs Related to Management Topics

All levels of managers should take advantage of certain computer software programs that are available. Knowledge of these programs may provide the reader with a competitive edge over those vying for his or her position. Several current programs covering practical management topics such as planning of projects, employee performance reviews, and business goals, are briefly described below. (Note: Some programs are similar in capability—for example, *Review Writer* and *Performance Now*—and the choice is yours.)

Fast Track Schedule 4.0 by AEC Software

This program uses a Gantt chart format and sets up a project with limitless phases and tasks. Activities are added by entering titles, start and finish dates, and durations. As activities are moved within a task list, they are arranged automatically in chronological order. Schedules may be formatted in a customized manner so they will provide the desired appearance for future activities and schedules. *Fast Track Schedule* offers a clean, detailed, and customized view of projects. It provides adequate reporting techniques for simple projects. (More complex projects may require more sophisticated reporting.) *Fast Track Schedule* is easy and straightforward to use, making it adequate for a middle manager.

DecideRight by Avantos Performance Systems, Inc.

This program enables you and your team to make tough decisions quickly, such as evaluating a purchase, choosing candidates for a company position, or buying a new computer.

For example, suppose you need to choose a new employee from several applicants, the program assists you through the following steps: (1) stating the ultimate decision relative to the position; (2)

entering the options you're considering, such as names of the finalists; (3) inputting criteria (such as experience, graduate degree, and salary requirements); (4) weighing the criteria; and (5) rating the options. The decision is calculated and the best candidate is selected by the program.

ManagePro 3.1 by Avantos Performance Systems, Inc.

This program allows you to set goals, track projects, keep track of appointments, and manage people by entering information into spreadsheet planners. *ManagePro* automatically generates color-coded status boards, schedules, and reports alerting you to what needs your attention. It will assist you in planning, keeping track of your goals, and providing useful feedback for your team.

More than 30 standard report types are accessible, and an unlimited amount of custom reports can be created.

Review Writer by Avantos Performance Systems, Inc.

This program provides you with an easy-to-use method for writing high quality appraisals, and walks you through every step of writing the review. It permits you to rate employees on performance factors either selected from the program or created by you. *Review Writer* provides standard text (based on your ratings), drawing from thousands of professionally written paragraphs that are contained within its software. You may edit the text and personalize it with specific examples that you may have logged in previously. Its Performance Log allows for entry of performance notes throughout the year. Performance Factor and Goal Raters permit evaluation of employees in appropriate performance areas for comprehensive appraisals.

TELEform by Cardiff Software

This automated forms processing system has the speed and accuracy needed to automatically collect data from scanned, faxed, or electronic forms. It reads hand-printed or typed data. Having data entered automatically helps increase productivity by capturing more data faster and with less effort on the user's part. Also, it allows you to use existing forms or to create custom forms. *TELE-form* stores information in the format that is best suited to your database, spreadsheet, or mainframe application.

AnyTime Deluxe by Individual Software

You can organize your contacts and meetings with *AnyTime Deluxe*. This program lets you create and send e-mail, organize personal and professional appointments as well as contact information. It also tracks tasks and action items and helps with keeping a journal, recording expenses and handling other routine duties. It permits printout of calendars, quick-formatted letters, and other documents.

Quicken 7.0 & Quicken Deluxe 7.0 by Intuit

Quicken organizes financial matters effectively. It prints checks, schedules bill payments, and reconciles bank accounts. With its reporting and graphics techniques, it will keep you apprised of where your money is disbursed and keeps track of your balance. It automatically sets up budgets based on data entry and helps track expenditures.

In the *Deluxe* form, this program can provide tracking of tax deductions, develop debt reduction plans, and assist in the selection of mutual funds. Furthermore, it can obtain news and quotations from Dow Jones and Standard & Poor's, and provide, five-year price charts on selected stock.

Schedule Insight by Kalyn Corp.

Schedule Insight helps keep your team informed and your schedules on track when used in conjunction with *Microsoft Project*. It provides the ability to access, analyze, and report project information whenever needed. The program automatically scrolls multiple projects and partitions them into simple tables by tasks, individuals, departments, and projects. More than 30 built-in report formats are available, or custom reports may be created.

With this program, team members can quickly locate their own tasks while managers and those in higher-level positions can get summaries of departmental and overall company activities.

Performance Now (Enterprise Edition) by KnowledgePoint

This software program is used for employee performance reviews. Employees are evaluated by using a standardized criteria, avoiding biasing. The program lets you develop organizational forms or design your own forms that will satisfy departmental needs. You can analyze trends by extracting past and present review data. Some of its features include: setting standards for performance reviews, rating employee performance chosen from 30 elements, assigning performance criteria and statistics, creating custom forms for different job categories, printing work sheets for employee self-review, and coaching ideas for improving employee performance.

Microsoft Project by Microsoft Corp.

This program aids in planning a project by allowing the user to enter deadline dates, which in turn automatically triggers other important dates for the duration of the project. It also permits switching from long-term planning using Gantt charts to monthly calendars. It is integrated with e-mail systems to automatically communicate tasks, assignments, and schedule changes for your team.

Timeslips Deluxe 7.0 by Timeslips Corp.

Timeslips is a program that tracks project-related activities and expenses, which are tallied on clients' bills, making it a more efficient way to monitor your business activities.

Most every client is different, and sometimes specific billing arrangements may be required for unique situations. This program provides several billing options such as: (1) flat fee arrangements; (2) tracking billable hours for meetings and phone conversations on a per minute basis; (3) tracking jobs by phases when "percent complete" billing is established; and (4) task-based billing. Other billing features include assessing interest and taxes, and maintaining a client's funds account.

Report outputs include: aged accounts receivable, client history, profit or loss based on flat fees; budgets; time analysis to track the performance of employees, activities, and clients, among others.

INDEX